SECOND
TIMOTHY

By

D. EDMOND HIEBERT

MOODY PRESS

CHICAGO

Contents

Preface

THIS SLENDER VOLUME on II Timothy offers a concise interpretation of the contents of this last letter from the apostle Paul. The reader is urged to keep a copy of the scriptural text open before him. The text quoted is that of the American Standard Version (1901), but the interpretation is based on a study of the original Greek. An attempt has been made to keep technical matters in connection with the original language to a minimum, and all Greek words, whenever quoted, have been transliterated into the English.

The material constitutes a verse-by-verse interpretation of the entire epistle, but the material is not cast into the form of comments on the verses seriatim. An outline, which it is hoped will serve as a chart and guide to its contents, has been inserted into the text of the interpretation in an effort to keep the trend of the apostle's thought clearly before the reader. Homiletical applications have been sparingly introduced, due to limitations of space.

My obligations to others will be evident from the Bibliography. In the exposition, quotations from various volumes on II Timothy are identified by the author's name, usually in parentheses, and refer to his discussion of the verse under consideration.

An Introduction to II Timothy

THE SECOND EPISTLE TO TIMOTHY has that peculiar appeal which belongs to the last known words of a great and beloved man. It was written with the full consciousness that "the time of his departure" was at hand. It constitutes Paul's dying testimony and his parting appeal to his beloved son in the Gospel. It has well been called Paul's "last will and testament to Timothy," and through him to the Church.

The impact that this last loving and impassioned appeal from his beloved teacher and guide had upon Timothy in his position of loneliness and grave peril cannot well be adequately imagined. What comfort, encouragement, inspiration, and new resolves must have flooded the heart of its devoted reader as, doubtless with tear-dimmed eyes, he read the affectionate admonitions, the stirring appeals, and the glorious promises of this epistle! And down through the centuries this priceless epistle has continued its blessed ministry to countless weary hearts and fiercely tested workers by imparting new strength and courage in the face of sorrow and persecution, administering needed consolation amid poignant loneliness and cravings for spiritual fellowship with loved ones, and inspiring new assurance of ultimate victory in facing seemingly insuperable obstacles and relentless forces of evil.

Second Timothy is the most personal of the Pastoral Epistles. The First Epistle to Timothy and that to Titus are more official in tone and content, having more largely in view the people with whom they were dealing as the apostolic representative. Second Timothy is personal throughout, a communication directed to the recipient himself. Far from being sentimental, it breathes the tenderness of a strong, heroic heart.

Even those critics who reject the Pauline authorship of the Pastoral Epistles feel compelled to admit the presence of "genuine fragments" in them, and especially in II Timothy. These critics postulate that some brief notes from Paul, most likely addressed to Timothy and Titus, had fallen into the hands of a later admirer of Paul, and that using these fragments as a nucleus, he composed the present epistles and issued them in the name of Paul. But the contents of II Timothy especially are so eminently characteristic of Paul that to attribute them to some later fabricator, say in the middle of the second century, who thus skillfully wove these fragments into his own work in clever imitation of the apostle, requires a great amount of credulity. Any person who could forge II Timothy in the style of Paul must have been a genius indeed! But nothing that has come down to us from the literature of the second century gives us any hope to believe that such literary ability existed. We fully agree with Farrar when he says:

> For myself I can only express my astonishment that anyone, who is sufficiently acquainted with the Christian literature of the first two centuries to see how few writers there were who showed a power even distantly capable of producing such a letter, can feel any hesitation as to its having been written by the hand of Paul.[1]

The united testimony of the early Church as well as the divine glow of its contents leave no room to doubt the authenticity of this matchless, inimitable epistle.

---

[1] F. W. Farrar, *The Life and Work of St. Paul,* (1889), p. 664.

Paul was a prisoner in Rome when he wrote II Timothy. He refers to himself as the Lord's prisoner (1:8), mentions the fact that he is chained (1:16), and says that he is suffering "hardship unto bonds, as a malefactor" (2:9). That he is in Rome is evident from the statement that Onesiphorus had visited him "when he was in Rome" (1:17).

But II Timothy cannot be grouped with the "Prison Epistles" (Colossians, Philemon, Ephesians, and Philippians), which were written during Paul's imprisonment mentioned in Acts 28. The historical conditions reflected in this epistle make it evident that it was written subsequent to the time of the Acts 28 imprisonment. It is generally conceded that the historical references contained in the Pastoral Epistles cannot be fitted into the story of Paul's life as given in Acts. The situation reflected in II Timothy is quite different from that of Acts 28 and points to a second Roman imprisonment as the time for this epistle. During the imprisonment in Acts 28 Paul was treated with considerable indulgence by the Roman government, being permitted to live "in his own hired dwelling" (v. 30); now he is kept in close confinement and regarded as a "malefactor" (1:16; 2:9). Then he was surrounded by a considerable circle of co-workers and friends (Acts 28:17-31; Col. 4:10-14; Phil. 1:13, 14); now he is almost alone (4:11) and former friends are turning from him (1:15). During the Acts 28 imprisonment he was freely accessible to all who wished to see him (v. 30); now even Onesiphorus could find him only after diligent search and at personal risk (1:16, 17). Then, as seen from the Prison Epistles, Paul confidently expected to be released (Phil. 1:25, 26; 2:24; Philemon 22); now he is looking forward to death, convinced that his end has come (4:6-8). Thus the situation reflected in

II Timothy is vastly different from that during the first Roman imprisonment.

These differences are best and most simply explained in the view that Paul experienced two imprisonments in Rome. Evidently Paul was released from the first Roman imprisonment. The Prison Epistles expect it, tradition asserts it, and the Pauline authorship of the Pastoral Epistles demands it. After some further missionary labors, due to a change of attitude toward Christianity on the part of the Roman government, Paul was again apprehended and imprisoned in Rome. II Timothy obviously belongs to the time following the edict of Nero against the Christians.

In July A.D. 64 a great fire destroyed a large part of the city of Rome. Well-founded rumors freely circulated in the devastated city that the fire had been ordered by Nero himself. Through various relief efforts Nero unsuccessfully sought to remove the odium of suspicion from himself. In a final desperate effort to clear himself Nero charged his incendiarism upon the Christians. The resultant savage Neronian persecutions, beginning apparently in October of that year, witnessed the death of hundreds of Christians by means of hideous martyrdoms. Christianity was made suspect and charged with being an enemy of the State. The attitude of the Emperor toward Christianity was quickly taken up by the enemies of Christianity and waves of persecution soon spread to the provinces.

It is not known where Paul was when he was again arrested, but Rome, Corinth, Nicopolis, and Troas have been suggested. Paul had left his precious books and parchments, materials vitally necessary for his missionary labors, at Troas (4:13), suggesting that his departure from there had been hasty and perhaps involuntary. From this it may be conjectured that Troas was the place of arrest.

8

Paul's case was transferred to Rome, where he suffered privation and close confinement as a dangerous individual, accused of being an enemy of the State. The time was a time of terror and danger for Christianity, and one by one his friends left him until he was almost alone (4:11). His loneliness in prison had been relieved by the courageous visits and ministries of the Ephesian Onesiphorus. Intense gratitude filled Paul's heart for this kindness (1:16-18).

When Paul's trial came up before the imperial court, he was accused of a capital crime. Paul appealed to certain notable Christian men in Asia, men familiar with his work and character, to come and testify in his behalf. But because of the hostile attitude of the government, the apparent hopelessness of the situation, and the personal dangers involved, they all avoided the risks involved in espousing his cause (1:15). Men like Luke and Timothy could not be called upon in this capacity, since as Paul's associates and assistants they had aided and abetted him in the alleged crime. The result was that at his first trial not a single friend had the courage to stand by his side to encourage him and to plead his cause. Paul courageously took up his own defense before the high tribunal, pleading his own cause. "As in the court of Felix and at his examination before Agrippa, his defense was a statement of the Gospel which he preached, defining its true nature and showing that it was no seditious propaganda."[2] His bold confrontation of his enemies, repelling every accusation against him, left its impression on the judges. His successful defense made a verdict of guilty impossible. He was remanded to prison and the case was adjourned for further study by the court (4:16, 17). Although he had escaped imminent danger of death, he knew that the too-

---

[2] David Smith, *The Life and Letters of St. Paul,* (no date), p. 626.

certain result had only been postponed. Under these circumstances he wrote this letter to Timothy.

The writing of the epistle was prompted by Paul's realization of the need of Timothy as well as his own yearning for the companionship of Timothy. Paul was led to write because of his fatherly concern for Timothy in that dark hour. Timothy was being torn with the memory of a dear past, shaken with the realization of a harrowing present, and oppressed with the gloomy prospect of an even darker future. While Timothy had wept an agony of tears (1:4) his beloved friend and teacher had been torn from him by the police or Roman soldiers. The hostility of the government toward Christianity had also cast an ominous cloud over Timothy as a Christian leader. He was exposed to fearful danger. Humanly speaking, the fury of the Neronian persecutions had left the Church trembling on the brink of extinction. The Roman Empire was intolerant of secret societies and it knew how to extinguish them. Only a clear vision of the divine destiny of the Church could foresee any other end. In such an hour to be prominent among the hated Christians might well mean that one was marked for destruction. For a timid soul the prospects were terrifying. "Timothy stood awfully lonely, yet awfully exposed, in the face of a world of thronging sorrows. Well might he be shaken to the root of his faith."[3] Knowing Timothy's natural timidity, Paul was concerned lest the threatening prospects should overwhelm him. Thus Paul wrote to him to rally his courage, to keep him steadfast in that dark hour, and to bid him be strong in the living Lord Jesus Christ. It is characteristic of both Paul and Timothy that in this hour the words of cheer and brave courage are being spoken by

[3] H.C.G. Moule, "The Second Epistle to Timothy," *A Devotional Commentary*, (1905 reprint), p. 14.
[4] F. W. Farrar, *The Life and Work of St. Paul*, (1889), p. 667.

the man facing imminent martyrdom rather than by the sorrowing young friend.

In the loneliness of his dark dungeon the heart of Paul craved the joy of the understanding and sympathetic presence of his beloved Timothy. That in the face of death Paul thus yearned for the fellowship of Timothy is eloquent testimony of the close relations between the two. As Farrar says:

> The very difference in their age, the very dissimilarity of their characters, had but made their love for each other more sacred and more deep. The ardent, impetuous, dominant character and intense purpose of the one, found its complement and its repose in the timid, yielding, retiring, character of the other.[4]

He writes to urge Timothy to come to him as soon as he can (4:21). He longs to be refreshed by the young man's devotion and to be cheered and comforted by his loving ministries.

The epistle also offered Paul an opportunity to record his own valedictory. Able to look back upon a life of devoted service to his precious Saviour and Lord, he can look death in the face unafraid. He can offer ringing testimony to the fact that in Christ the believer can be triumphant over life and death. In the face of impending martyrdom the apostle can utter his stirring testimony of Christian victory:

> I am already being offered, and the time of my departure is come. I have fought the good fight, I have finished the course, I have kept the faith: henceforth there is laid up for me the crown of righteousness, which the Lord, the righteous judge, shall give to me at that day; and not to me only, but also to all them that love his appearing (4:6-8).

These words may properly be regarded as Paul's epitaph.

Unlike I Timothy, II Timothy does not contain any

definite statement as to the place of Timothy's residence at the time of writing. The contents of the epistle, however, seem best to suit the conclusion that Timothy was at Ephesus or its vicinity.

The epistle must be dated only a few months before the death of Paul. The exact date assigned to it will depend upon the date accepted for Paul's martyrdom. Our reconstruction of the closing years of Paul's life, as drawn from the references in the Pastoral Epistles, leads us to suggest that II Timothy was written in the late summer or early autumn of A.D. 66. Whether or not Timothy arrived at Paul's side before his execution is not known.

An Outline of II Timothy

THE INTRODUCTION, 1:1-5
  1. *The Salutation,* vv. 1, 2
    a. The writer, v. 1
    b. The reader, v. 2a
    c. The greeting, v. 2b
  2. *The Expression of Gratitude,* vv. 3-5
    a. The statement of his gratitude, v. 3a
    b. The description of his feeling, vv. 3b-5
      1) His incessant remembrance of Timothy, v. 3b
      2) His yearning for Timothy, v. 4
      3) His reminder of Timothy's faith, v. 5

I. THE EXHORTATIONS TO STEADFASTNESS IN THE MINISTRY, 1:6—2:13
  1. *The Essential Qualities of the Steadfast Minister,* 1:6-18
    a. The zeal of the minister, vv. 6, 7
      1) The appeal for zeal, v. 6
      2) The incentive for zeal, v. 7
    b. The courage of the minister, vv. 8-12
      1) The appeal for courage, v. 8
      2) The incentive to courage, vv. 9-12
        a) The truths of the Gospel, vv. 9, 10
        b) The position and attitude of the apostle, vv. 11, 12
          i) His position in relation to the Gospel, v. 11
          ii) His attitude in suffering for the Gospel, v. 12

c. The fidelity of the minister, **vv.** 13-18
1) The appeal for fidelity, vv. 13, 14
a) The exhortation to hold the pattern of sound words, v. 13
b) The exhortation to guard the good deposit, v. 14
2) The incentive to fidelity, vv. 15-18
a) Neg.—the example of those in Asia, v. 15
b) Pos.—the courageous example of Onesiphorus, vv. 16-18
i) The prayer for the house of Onesiphorus, v. 16a
ii) The services of Onesiphorus at Rome, vv. 16b, 17
iii) The prayer for Onesiphorus, v. 18a
iv) The ministry of Onesiphorus at Ephesus, v. 18b
2. *The Duties of the Steadfast Minister*, 2:1-13
a. The duty of personal strengthening, v. 1
b. The duty of transmitting the truth, v. 2
c. The duty of steadfast endurance for the Gospel, vv. 3-13
1) The demand for endurance in the Christian life, vv. 3-7
a) The call to suffer hardship as a good soldier, v. 3
b) The pictures of the Christian life, vv. 4-6
i) The picture of the soldier, v. 4
ii) The picture of the athlete, v. 5
iii) The picture of the farmer, v. 6
c) The duty to understand the pictures, v. 7
2) The motivation for endurance in the Christian life, vv. 8-13

a) The constant remembrance of Jesus Christ, v. 8

b) The suffering of Paul in the Gospel, vv. 9, 10

c) The certainty of the future reward, vv. 11-13

II. THE EXHORTATIONS TO DOCTRINAL SOUNDNESS, 2:14—4:8

1. *The Minister's Reaction to Doctrinal Error,* 2:14-26

a. The urgent activity amid doctrinal error, vv. 14-19

1) The nature of the activity, vv. 14-16a

a) His warning against doctrinal error, v. 14

b) His example as a master-workman, v. 15

c) His shunning of profane babblings, v. 16a

2) The reasons for the activity, vv. 16b-19

a) Because of the destructive effect of error, vv. 16b-18

b) Because of the demand of divine truth, v. 19

b. The needed holiness of life amid doctrinal error, vv. 20-26

1) The picture of the mixed condition in the "great house," vv. 20, 21

a) The two types of utensils in the house, v. 20

b) The needed separation for a position of honor, v. 21

2) The application to the minister's work, vv. 22-26

a) The exhortation to personal purity of life, v. 22

b) The command to disdain foolish and ignorant questions, v. 23

An Outlined Interpretation
of II Timothy

THE INTRODUCTION, 1:1-5

Paul, an apostle of Christ Jesus through the will of God, according to the promise of life which is in Christ Jesus, to Timothy, my beloved child: Grace, mercy, peace, from God the Father and Christ Jesus our Lord.

I thank God, whom I serve from my forefathers in a pure conscience, how unceasing is my remembrance of thee in my supplications, night and day longing to see thee, remembering thy tears, that I may be filled with joy; having been reminded of the unfeigned faith that is in thee; which dwelt first in thy grandmother Lois, and thy mother Eunice; and, I am persuaded, in thee also.

THE INTRODUCTION to II Timothy is characteristically Pauline. It opens with the usual Pauline salutation with its distinctively Christian form and connotations (vv. 1, 2). This is followed, in accordance with Paul's practice, by a statement of his gratitude to God for the reader, a statement full of deep emotional overtones (vv. 3-5).

1. *The Salutation,* vv. 1, 2

The salutation is very similar to that in I Timothy, yet there are interesting differences in the details. Each of the three members in this salutation receives some expansion, half of the brief salutation being devoted to the writer. As in I Timothy, the writer and reader are named once each, God the Father is mentioned twice, while the name of Christ Jesus is mentioned three times. How Paul loved and gloried in that adorable name! The very thought of Him runs through all of his thinking and writing. He cannot move, think, or live without Him. Truly for Paul "to live is Christ" (Phil. 1:21).

a. The writer, v. 1. In accordance with the accepted practice of that day, Paul begins with his own name. We moderns sign our name at the end of our letters, while the writer of a letter in that day, with greater logic, placed his name at the beginning of his letter. And the very sight of that name at the head of this communication to him must have thrilled the soul of Timothy. How eagerly he would peruse any word from his beloved friend and teacher!

The writer describes himself as "an apostle of Christ Jesus through the will of God." At first sight it may seem rather strange that Paul in this personal communication to his beloved son Timothy should thus insist upon his apostleship. The stress upon it is not due to any need for its defense. Rather, everything that Paul writes to Timothy is in the interest of that apostleship. It is in his office as a God-commissioned apostle that he writes this letter to his son who will soon have the responsibility to carry on alone the cause of the Lord. His apostolic authority enforces all that he has to say to Timothy. "Intimacy was never meant to enfeeble that divinely given place and authorty" (Kelly).

His official position is that of "an apostle." The term "apostle," coming from the Greek verb *apostellō*, means "one who is sent forth or dispatched on a mission" and carries the thought of official and authoritative sending with the necessary equipment for the commission received. In the New Testament the term is sometimes used in a broad sense to designate an official messenger or representative (cf. II Cor. 8:23; Phil. 2:25). Here, however, Paul uses the term in its usual narrow sense as one called to the apostolic office, like the Twelve, and invested with its authority. The added genitive "of Christ Jesus" defines whose apostle he is. He belongs to Christ, has been commissioned and sent by Him, and acts as His authorized representative.

The Greek manuscripts vary in the order of the compound name. The order "Christ Jesus," followed in the American Standard Version, has much stronger support than the reverse order in the King James Version. Both orders are common to Paul, but the order "Christ Jesus," while not prominent in his earlier epistles, gradually takes over until in the Pastoral Epistles it is the prevailing order used.[1]

The average English reader uses either order merely to designate the Person to whom reference is being made without a clear sense of any difference in meaning. But to Paul and his Greek readers each order had a significance over and above that of a mere identification of the Person. In either case the first member of the compound name indicated whether the theological or the historical idea was uppermost in the writer's mind.

[1] In the Greek text of E. Nestle "Christ Jesus" occurs twenty-five times while "Jesus Christ" occurs six times in the Pastoral Epistles.

The word "Christ" is a transliteration of the Greek word *christos* and is the equivalent of the Hebrew word translated "Messiah," both meaning "the anointed one." On the opening pages of the Gospels "the Christ" is not a personal name but an official designation for the expected Messiah (cf. Matt. 2:4; Luke 3:15). As by faith the human Jesus was recognized and accepted as the personal Messiah, the article was dropped and the designation came to be used as a personal name. The name "Christ" speaks of His Messianic dignity and emphasizes that He is the fulfillment of the Old Testament promises concerning the coming Messiah. The name "Jesus," the other member of the compound designation, comes from the Greek *Iēsous,* the Greek form of the Hebrew name "Joshua," which means "Jehovah saves." It was the name given Him by the angel before He was born (Luke 1:31; Matt. 1:21). It is His human name and speaks of the fact of His Incarnation, His taking upon Himself human form to become our Saviour.

The order "Jesus Christ" places the emphasis on the historical appearing of the man Jesus who by faith was recognized and acknowledged as the Messiah. It proclaims the fact that "Jesus is the Christ." It speaks of Him who came in human form, became obedient unto death, and was afterward exalted and glorified. This order is always followed in the epistles of Peter, John, James, and Jude.[2] Perhaps this is because in the experience of these writers the human life of Jesus came first in their experiences with our Lord.

The order "Christ Jesus" points to the theological fact that the One who was with the Father in eternal glory became incarnate in human form. This order is peculiar to Paul. Perhaps this is due to the fact that Paul's first per-

2 The critical texts omit the name "Jesus" in I Peter 5:10, 14.

22

sonal encounter with Him was as the Christ in Glory. Thus Erdman remarks:

> While the other apostles had known their Master first as a man and later as a Messiah, it may be that for this reason they called him Jesus Christ, while Paul, whose first vision was of the glorified Lord, always thought of him as the divine Christ who had borne the human name of Jesus, and whom Paul loved and adored as Christ Jesus.

By calling himself "an apostle of Christ Jesus" Paul stresses the fact that the Person who had called and commissioned him to be His messenger was the Christ of glory who had been ordained and anointed by God in His Incarnation to procure the salvation of His people.

Paul accounts for his apostleship by indicating that he is such "through the will of God." He was an apostle because God in His sovereignty had willed it. He was not an apostle by personal choice; it was a divine entrustment. His apostleship was not of human origin, nor of human ordination, but came to him directly from Christ (Gal. 1:1). In I Timothy 1:1 he mentions that his apostleship was "according to the commandment of God" and as such had to be obeyed. In four other epistles, as here, he relates his apostleship to the will of God (I Cor. 1:1; II Cor. 1:1; Eph. 1:1; Col. 1:1). It was the consciousness that the divine will had chosen him as an apostle, although he neither sought nor merited it, that held him firm throughout all the years of his strenuous and eventful life. It was this conviction that kept him calm in the face of impending martyrdom. As a prisoner, lonely and largely forsaken, he could fall back upon the consciousness that "he is an apostle, not by his own appointment, but by the will of God. In the hour of our extremity, when earthly friends and securities fail, there is but one security, the rock on which we stand, *the will of God,* and the assurance that we are standing upon it" (Horton).

Paul further characterizes his office as being "according to the promise of the life which is in Christ Jesus." The significance of this phrase has been differently interpreted. It is generally held that the words are to be referred back to the word "apostle," rather than taken with what immediately precedes. This is the view adopted in the King James as well as in the American Standard Version, as shown by the use of a comma after the word "God." This interprets the expression as denoting "the object or intention of his appointment as apostle, which was to make known, to publish abroad, the promise of eternal life" (Spence). But we feel that it is far simpler to take the phrase in close connection with the whole of what precedes. The preposition (*kata*) retains its ordinary sense of "according to, in conformity or harmony with." His apostleship by the will of God was in perfect harmony with "the promise of life," that is, the promise which had life as its contents. "Had there been no such promise there could have been no divinely willed apostle to proclaim the promise" (Hendriksen). The words thus express not the object and intention of the apostleship but rather its character as being in harmony with God's promise of life. The apostleship of Paul certainly did further the proclamation of the promise of eternal life, but the thought here is that his apostleship was in harmony with that promise.

The promised life is described as that "which is in Christ Jesus." It is not simply life but that God-promised life "in union with Christ Jesus." It is "life in the higher sense, comprehensive of all the blessings and glory, both in this world and the next, which flow from an interest in the redemption of Christ" (Fairbairn). And it is only in union with Christ that this life is available to man. "He that hath the Son hath the life; he that hath not the Son of God hath not the life" (I John 5:12). How appropriate that Paul in facing imminent martyrdom should cling to this life in Christ which no temporal death is able to harm!

b. The reader, v. 2a. The letter is addressed "to Timothy, my beloved child." In the salutation of I Timothy Paul addresses him as "my true [genuine] child in faith" (1:2), thus clearly implying that Timothy was Paul's own convert. He was not a spurious son but a genuine child. Paul's use of the word "child" (*teknon*) is full of fatherly tenderness, a fact which the rendering "son" in the King James Version does not convey. He is further designated as "my *beloved* child." (The "my" is implied but not expressed in the Greek.) The adjective "beloved" indicates intelligent and purposeful love for Timothy on the part of his spiritual father. "The whole letter throbs with the love of a father for a beloved child" (Lenski). Since Paul is quite aware that this letter may in reality be his farewell to his devoted young friend, his fatherly heart goes out to him in tender love and solicitude.

It is highly arbitrary for Alford to hold that Paul's use of the term "beloved," instead of "true" as in the first epistle, expresses "more of mere love, and less of confidence, than in the former." That Timothy does not now deserve the former epithet of confidence is discredited by Paul's reference to the "unfeigned faith" of Timothy (v.5). The term of affection is appropriate here since this letter is written under the shadow of the impending crisis of Paul's martyrdom. As Van Oosterzee remarks: "It was not so much in the mind of the Apostle to bear honorable witness to Timothy, as to express the inwardness of the relation in which both stood to each other."

c. The greeting, v. 2b. "Grace, mercy, peace, from

God the Father and Christ Jesus our Lord." This greeting is identical to that found in I Timothy. Both are unusual in that "mercy" is inserted between the familiar "grace and peace." Such a threefold invocation of blessing upon the reader occurs elsewhere in the epistles only in II John 3, written years later.[3] A second-century forger of these epistles would not have dared to make such a striking departure from the usual practice of Paul in the very opening of his composition. But it is very natural that the keen solicitude and loving concern of the apostle for his timid and troubled young friend should lead him to insert this added prayer for mercy upon Timothy. It adds that tender personal touch that Timothy needed.

This beautiful triple invocation invokes upon Timothy all the blessings which are offered to us now through the Gospel of Christ. "Grace" is the undeserved favor of God toward the guilty sinner, flowing out in divine goodness and removing the guilt of his past sins and relieving him of deserved punishment. "Mercy" is the self-moved, spontaneous loving-kindness of God which causes Him to deal in compassion and tender affection with the miserable and distressed, freeing the sinner from the resultant misery of his sins. "Peace" is the state of salvation and spiritual well-being which results from the experience of God's grace and mercy. It is the outcome of the restoration of harmony between the soul and God upon the basis of the atoning work of Christ.

Paul thinks of this triad of blessings as coming "from God the Father and Christ Jesus our Lord." Both are involved in the bestowal of these gifts. They come from Him who, as the author of our salvation, holds the relation of Father to all believers because of their union by

---

[3] The word "mercy" is rightly omitted in Titus 1:4 as lacking sufficient manuscript authority.

26

faith with His Son. They also come from the Son who through His redemptive work made possible the bestowal of grace, mercy, and peace. Having been redeemed by Him, believers accept His authority over their lives and acknowledge Him as "Lord." Paul uses the appropriative pronoun "our" to indicate that he and Timothy alike accept Christ Jesus as Lord.

The union of the two Persons under the government of the one preposition "from" is strong circumstantial evidence concerning Paul's faith in the true deity of Christ Jesus. It would have been unthinkable for Paul, with his strong monotheistic background, thus to have associated the name of Jesus with that of God if he did not believe in His deity.

It is interesting to notice the resemblances as well as the differences in the salutations of the two letters addressed to Timothy. These will be readily apparent when we place them in parallel columns and italicize the words that differ.

I Timothy 1:1,2	II Timothy 1:1,2
Paul, an apostle of Christ Jesus *according to the commandment* of God *our Saviour, and* Christ Jesus *our hope;* unto Timothy, my *true* child *in faith*: Grace, mercy, peace, from God the Father and Christ Jesus our Lord.	Paul, an apostle of Christ Jesus *through the will* of God, *according to the promise of the life which is in* Christ Jesus, to Timothy, my *beloved* child: Grace, mercy, peace, from God the Father and Christ Jesus our Lord.

Such a comparison leads Williams aptly to remark:

> There are two conclusions lying right on the surface: The second Letter is not a copy of the first, nor is either a copy of a common source. Again, the thought is so nearly the same that the Pauline authorship could not be asserted for one and denied for the other.

27

2. *The Expression of Gratitude,* vv. 3-5.

To the salutation Paul adds a word of sincere and heartfelt gratitude to God on behalf of Timothy. These three verses form one involved sentence and have been the occasion of much discussion and not a little disagreement among the scholars.

Much of the difficulty arises out of the common practice of taking the opening words of the original, *charin echō tō theō,* to mean "I thank God," as in our versions. This naturally leads to the question, For what does Paul give thanks? Different parts of the sentence have been regarded as the subject of the thanksgiving. The usual view is to regard the "unfeigned faith" of verse 5 as that for which Paul gives thanks, while the intermediate phrases are regarded as a sort of parenthesis giving the circumstances under which it is displayed. But quite literally Paul says, "Gratitude I am having to God." Since he is recording his feeling of gratitude he needs no objective statement of the thing for which he gives thanks. All that follows, namely, all of his treasured memories of Timothy, describes his feeling of gratitude. Thus viewed, Paul expresses the fact of his gratitude (v. 3a) and gives a description of his gratitude to God (vv. 3b-5).

a. The statement of his gratitude, v. 3a. The words here translated "I thank God" are not Paul's usual formula of thanksgiving. Usually he says *eucharistō tō theō* (Rom. 1:8; I Cor. 1:4; Phil. 1:3; Col. 1:3; I Thess. 1:2; II Thess. 1:3; Philemon 4). The expression here used occurs elsewhere in Paul's writings only in I Timothy 1:12. (It occurs elsewhere in the New Testament only in Luke 17:9 and Heb. 12:28.) Literally rendered Paul says, "Gratitude I am having to God." The present tense of the verb indicates the gratitude as a continuing fact. His heart is full of gratitude to God as the flood of his memories concerning Timothy crowd in upon his soul.

His relationship to God, to whom his gratitude ascends, is indicated in the phrase, "whom I serve from my forefathers in a pure conscience." The verb rendered "serve" denotes the rendering of religious service or worship to God and was the word used to indicate the worship of Jehovah by the covenant people of God. The God whom he is serving he learned to know from his forefathers. By forefathers he apparently means his immediate ancestors rather than the national ancestors Abraham, Isaac, and Jacob, whom he generally designates as "the fathers" (Rom. 9:5, etc.). Paul came from a line of ancestors who, as members of the covenant nation, were sincere, godly people and worshiped the true God according to the light that they had. His forefathers had passed on to him the knowledge of the true God, and this God he now continues to serve "in a pure conscience." It was the atmosphere in which his service was rendered. He may be accused of teaching a new, strange, and illegal god in the empire, who could not be worshiped with a pure conscience because forbidden by law, but the God whom he is serving is the same God his forefathers have served and is even now officially recognized as the God of the Jewish people throughout the Roman Empire. Paul has not changed his worship, but it is Rome that has changed. Paul was deeply convinced that Christianity was the true continuation and development, yea, the culmination of the Old Testament revelation. In holding to his faith as a Christian he had not denied his former faith or the faith of his ancestors (Acts 24:14-16; 26:6-7; Rom. 11:13-24; Gal. 3:7-29). Although a prisoner on behalf of the Gospel, his conscience is clear as he approaches God in his dungeon.

b. The description of his feeling, vv. 3b-5. He proceeds to set forth his memories concerning Timothy which prompt his feeling of gratitude to God. The passage is laden with the thought of those memories, three different words being employed to refer to them. As he faces the end of his own life his mind goes back and dwells on the memories that he treasures in connection with his beloved Timothy. He speaks of his incessant remembrance of him (v. 3b), his yearning for him (v. 4), and his reminder of Timothy's faith (v. 5).

1) His incessant remembrance of Timothy, v. 3b. "How unceasing is my remembrance of thee in my supplications." The Greek word here translated "how" (*hōs*) has been variously rendered and the context must decide the preferable translation. The "how" of the American Standard Version implies that the cause for thanksgiving is the unceasing nature of Paul's recollections of Timothy, while the "that" in the King James Version refers the cause to the remembrance itself. It seems best here to retain its usual significance of "as, just as, even as." We then translate quite literally, "Even as I am having unceasing remembrance concerning you in my supplications." By saying "even as" Paul indicates that whenever he thinks of his beloved Timothy he thinks of him as likewise serving the true God with a pure conscience. He cherishes a constant recollection "concerning" (*peri*) him. Lenski observes: "'Concerning thee' does not refer merely to Timothy's person, but to the circumstances surrounding Timothy, which induce Paul to petition God to help Timothy in this and that matter." And this he does in his "supplications" for him. The word implies a realization of need and a petition for its supply. These petitions Paul offers "night and day." The punctuation in the American Standard Version connects these words

30

with verse 4, but it seems best here, as in I Timothy 5:5, to connect them with what precedes. Some of Paul's prayers are being offered during the long hours of the night in his dark dungeon, while other prayers for Timothy ascend to God during the day. (Paul always uses this order.) These words give us a glimpse into the unwearied practice of intercession by Paul, and Timothy was given a prominent place in it. "It is good to pray for individuals; it is good also to tell them that you pray for them" (Horton).

2) His yearning for Timothy, v. 4. "Longing to see thee." Accompanying and at least in part occasioning his supplications for Timothy is his deep, continued longing to see Timothy again. The word is expressive of the natural yearning of personal affection. "He loved Timothy as a man loves his own son; and he longed for the joy of renewed fellowship with him face to face" (Lilley). The force of the original construction marks the direction of the desire; it is for Timothy that he yearns. That yearning is nourished by his constant remembrance of Timothy's tears. He does not specify the occasion for those tears, but the context implies that it was the bitterness of parting from his revered leader, apparently at Paul's last arrest, that caused the tears. They were genuine tears of love and concern as his spiritual father was being torn from him. Stimulated by this memory, Paul longs for reunion, "that I may be filled with joy." To see Timothy again would be joy indeed. "Paul's memories afford him great joy as he sits in his dismal dungeon, but once more to get to see Timothy, his beloved Timothy, will fill Paul's cup of joy to the very brim. Gratitude is coupled with anticipated joy" (Lenski).

3) His reminder of Timothy's faith, v. 5. "Having been reminded of the unfeigned faith that is in thee." The

Greek word used here, Paul's third reference to his memories, denotes an external reminding. The "call to remembrance" of the King James does not adequately give the force of the word. The occasion for this reminding is not indicated, but something had happened at Rome under Paul's eyes which strongly reminded him of Timothy's faith. It is a gracious hint to his young friend, indicating to him "how Paul esteems Timothy's faith, considers it a model, with which sincere acts of other men's faith are compared in Paul's mind" (Lenski).

Timothy's faith is given a twofold description. It is "unfeigned," literally, "unhypocritical"; a faith arising out of an inner reality of conviction and knowing no sham or pretense. It is further described by the clause "which [lit., *which is such as*] dwelt first in thy grandmother Lois, and thy mother Eunice." Timothy is parallel to Paul in that he too has a line of godly ancestors, in whom this "unhypocritical faith" has effectively taken up its abode.

Views have differed as to what Paul meant by the "faith" of Lois and Eunice. Was it nothing more than the devout faith of the true Israelite in the scriptural promises of the coming Messiah, or was it personal faith in Jesus Christ? Doubtless both meanings must be included. Both the mother and the grandmother had been devout Israelites adhering to the true faith of their people as grounded in and nurtured by the Old Testament Scriptures. From them Timothy has inherited the knowledge of the true God, having received instruction in the Scriptures from childhood (3:14-17). But when the message of the Gospel of Jesus Christ was brought to them, their unfeigned faith led them to an open acceptance of Him. Scripture does not give the place and manner of their conversion. Moule thinks that "they were very probably 'original disciples' (see Acts 21:16), fruits, more or less

32

directly, of Pentecost itself," and later drawn to Paul. It is generally held that they were led to accept Christ during Paul's first missionary journey. Since Paul says this faith "first" dwelt in the grandmother, it would then appear that she first accepted Christ and then worked in co-operation with Paul in the conversion of Timothy. His mention of them by name indicates that both were personally known to Paul. And now as he reviews his memories of Timothy he is fully persuaded, or assured, that this same faith indwells Timothy also. "This is intended to cheer the depressed disciple, and suggests that whatever others may assert about Timothy, Paul is assured of his sincere godliness" (Pope).

I. THE EXHORTATIONS TO STEADFASTNESS IN THE MINISTRY, 1:6—2: 13

S ECOND TIMOTHY, written to encourage and fortify Timothy in that dark hour, is largely composed of a series of fervent appeals to Timothy from his spiritual father and loving friend. Although there are no formally marked divisions in the epistle, the earlier part presents exhortations to steadfastness in the ministry (1:6-2:13), while the remainder of the body of the letter relates to matters of doctrinal soundness (2:14-4:8). The exhortations to steadfastness deal with the essential qualities of the steadfast minister (1:6-18) and the duties of the steadfast minister (2:1-13).

1. *The Essential Qualities of the Steadfast Minister,* 1:6-18

For which cause I put thee in remembrance that thou stir up the gift of God, which is in thee through the laying on of my hands. For God gave us not a spirit of fearfulness; but of power and love and discipline. Be not ashamed therefore of the testimony of our Lord, nor of me his prisoner: but suffer hardship with the gospel according to the power of God; who saved us, and called us with a holy calling, not according to our works, but according to his own purpose and grace, which was given us in Christ Jesus before times eternal, but hath now been manifested by the appearing of our Saviour Christ Jesus, who abolished death, and brought life and immortality to light through the gospel, whereunto I was appointed a preacher, and an apostle, and a teacher. For which cause I suffer also these things: yet I am not ashamed; for I know him whom I have believed, and I am persuaded that he is able to guard that which I have committed unto him against that day. Hold the pattern of sound words which thou hast heard from me, in faith and love which is in Christ Jesus. That good thing which was committed unto thee guard through the Holy Spirit which dwelleth in us.

This thou knowest, that all that are in Asia turned away from me; of whom are Phygelus and Hermogenes. The Lord grant mercy unto the house of Onesiphorus: for he oft refreshed me, and was not ashamed of my chain; but, when he was in Rome, he sought me diligently, and found me (the Lord grant unto him to find mercy of the Lord in that day); and in how many things he ministered at Ephesus, thou knowest very well.

The exhortations of this section appeal for three essential qualities in the minister—his zeal (vv. 6, 7), his courage (vv. 8-12), and his fidelity (vv. 13-18). In each case the appeal is stated and the incentive added.

a. The zeal of the minister, vv. 6, 7. By saying "for which cause," Paul connects his exhortations with his own memories of and conviction concerning Timothy. On that basis he can confidently proceed with exhortation, pointing out to him what he will need to do now more than ever before. Paul's words "I put thee in remembrance," more literally, "I am reminding thee," tactfully represent Timothy as himself conscious of these duties which are now urged upon him. All that he needs is reminding. Paul makes an appeal for zeal (v. 6) and supplies an incentive (v. 7).

1) The appeal for zeal, v. 6. "That thou stir up the gift of God." It is an unwarranted inference to conclude from these words that Timothy has allowed his spiritual flame to die down. Such a view is inconsistent with Paul's statement in verse 5. It also overlooks the force of the present tense of the infinitive which means rather that Timothy is to keep the flame blazing at white heat as he has been doing. It is not an implied rebuke for neglect but a fatherly appeal bravely to continue in the face of serious difficulty. The appeal is preventative rather than corrective. The appeal is timely and pertinent in view of the development of imperial hostility to Christianity.

"The gift of God" which is to be kept blazing is doubtless the same gift mentioned in I Timothy 4:14. It is "the ministerial gift, including all the gifts for the sacred office, with special emphasis here, perhaps, on boldness in the faith" (Harvey). This gift is now in him "through the laying on of my hands." In I Timothy 4:14 reference was appropriately made to the part of the presbytery in its bestowal; in this personal communication Paul mentions only his own part therein. The usual view connects this with Timothy's ordination at Lystra (Acts 16:1-3). If we connect it with Ephesus, then it relates to the time when Timothy was installed into his Asian work as the apostolic representative.

2) The incentive for zeal, v. 7. The incentive for ministerial zeal lies in the "spirit" which God has given to us

as Christians. Some would interpret "spirit" here to mean the Holy Spirit. It seems better with our versions to regard the reference to the inner qualities, the spiritual character wrought in us by the Holy Spirit. This Spirit-wrought character, described negatively and positively, is the gift of God's grace. Negatively, it is "not a spirit of fearfulness." God did not give us a spirit of fearfulness, cowardice, or timidity, so that we cower and let our flame die down when confronted with the prospects of suffering. "But," on the contrary, God gave us a spirit "of power and love and discipline." These three graces are especially needed by one in Timothy's circumstances. Threatening clouds are rapidly darkening the sky; added to the prevailing local hostility to the planting and development of the Church there is now imperial hostility. In the face of these ominous developments there is need for "power," aggressive energy in the face of difficulty, which overcomes the weakness of cowardice and enables one to work, to endure, to suffer, and to die if need be. Needed also is the spirit "of love," that self-forgetting love to Christ, the church, and the souls of men, which exhorts, warns, rebukes with boldness and fidelity at whatever risk of consequences to self. The third quality mentioned is "discipline." The original word means "the act of making sober, or calling to soundness of mind." The translation "discipline" interprets it as referring to the act of disciplining or correcting others. The word may bear that meaning, but that seems out of harmony here with the other members of the trio which are personal graces, not official powers. The meaning is rather that of self-control, self-discipline, the exercise of a sane, balanced mind. "As Paul grew older and richer in experience, he realized the value to the preacher of religious sanity" (Greene).

b. The courage of the minister, vv. 8-12. "Therefore"

indicates that this second appeal is based on and follows out of the preceding statement of incentive. He states the appeal for courage (v. 8) and adds an incentive (vv. 9-12).

1) The appeal for courage, v. 8. The appeal is stated both negatively and positively. Negatively, "be not ashamed of the testimony of our Lord, nor of me his prisoner." "Be not ashamed" does not imply that he is; rather the construction in the original urges that he must not yield to the temptation to become ashamed. He must not give way to a feeling of shame and shrink from his duties in regard to "the testimony of our Lord." The reference is not to our Lord's personal testimony while here on earth. It is rather Timothy's witness to Christ and the message of the Gospel which has been committed to him. This is all the more necessary now that Christianity is regarded as an illegal religion. By saying "our Lord" Paul "contrasts Him with Caesar, whom his contemporaries were in the habit of so calling" (Pope). "Nor of me his prisoner" reminds Timothy that Paul is already feeling the wrath of the emperor but he is not ashamed to be known as a prisoner for the Lord's sake. As the Lord's prisoner Paul is confident that "whatever pertains to his incarceration was entirely safe in the hands of the Sovereign Disposer of destinies" (Hendriksen).

Positively, Timothy is urged to "suffer hardship with the Gospel." The compound verb does not strictly mean to suffer "hardship" but rather to suffer something bad or base, to suffer ill treatment. The rendering "suffer hardship with the Gospel" personifies the Gospel as actively suffering under the imperial persecution—a rather bold and startling figure since the Gospel does not actively suffer. It seems better to regard the preposition "with," in the compound verb, as associating Timothy with Paul in his sufferings for the Gospel. He must share with Paul in suffering "in the interest of the Gospel." But lest Timothy, naturally inclined to be timid, might feel that this made a demand beyond his abilities, Paul reminds him that the suffering is to be "according to the power of God." The reference may be either to the power which God imparts (v. 7) or the power which belongs to God and He has exhibited in our salvation (v. 9). From the context the latter reference seems preferable but surely both thoughts are involved. That power which God has displayed in working our own salvation He also imparts to us to be enabled to suffer for the Gospel. The test of our power lies in our ability to suffer for the Gospel.

2) The incentive to courage, vv. 9-12. A twofold incentive to courage is set before Timothy—the glorious truths of the Gospel of salvation (vv. 9-10) and the personal example of Paul's position and attitude (vv. 11, 12).

a) The truths of the Gospel, vv. 9, 10. By means of an articular participle construction, standing in apposition with the word "God," Paul continues without a break to set forth the glories of our divinely wrought salvation. It has its origin in eternity past in the purpose of God, received its manifestation in the work of the historic Christ, and finds its consummation in the immortality that carries us into eternal blessedness.

The author of this salvation is the God "who saved us, and called us with a holy calling." The words "saved" and "called" translate two aorist participles and indicate the actual result of the operation of the divine power in "us." By "us" Paul means himself and Timothy, but it includes all who are saved and called. In the epistles, the calling always denotes an effective and successful calling.

38

The order of the two terms, united under one article, is interesting. Boise observes:

As the order now stands, it presents the picture of one who is wandering away from God. He is stopped in his course. This first divine act saves him. He is then called, invited, with a holy calling—holy in contrast with the invitations to sin such as he had previously listened to.

The calling is the work of God's holiness and it leads to holiness in the called.

The fountainhead of this salvation Paul indicates both negatively and positively. Negatively, "not according to our works." "Our works were neither the consideration for which, nor the standard according to which, he saved and called us" (Harvey). Our works had not the least trace of holiness to merit His holy calling. This characteristically Pauline thought shows that the emphasis upon the importance of good works in the Pastoral Epistles is not inconsistent with Paul's doctrine of salvation. "But," on the contrary, our salvation is "according to his own purpose and grace." "His own" is emphatic. "He was self-moved, impelled by motives, not from without, but from within himself" (Harvey). Our salvation arises out of God's own "purpose and grace." Only God's sovereign and wise purpose is the norm for our salvation. If our salvation depended on our own deserving, we might well despair, but it has its ground in God's eternal and unshakable purpose. And that purpose expressed itself in "grace," the unmerited favor of God toward us guilty sinners. This grace is described as that "which was given us in Christ Jesus before times eternal." By speaking of this grace as "given us . . . before times eternal," Paul traces our salvation back into eternity past. Although we were still non-existent, in the eternal mind of God this grace was given us "in Christ Jesus," in virtue of our union with Him. "Christ and his body, the church, are one and indivisible in the divine mind, and grace was given to the chosen, therefore, where in eternity they were chosen in him" (Harvey). This gift of grace "before times eternal," prior to the time when the successive ages of time began to run their course, was the actualization of God's idea of that which he had purposed in Himself.

This grace "hath now been manifested by the appearing of our Saviour Christ Jesus." Here the apostle returns to the sphere of time. Over against the purpose of God from all eternity he sets the historical manifestation of His grace in the appearing of Christ Jesus in human history. Both the verb "manifested" and the noun "appearing," which have the same root, express the thought of making plain or bringing into view that which was previously hidden. The "appearing" or "epiphany" of Christ refers to His Incarnation and His entire earthly ministry. (Only here does Paul use the word "epiphany" of Christ's First Advent). The title "our Saviour" emphasizes the saving purpose of His manifestation in incarnation and our personal appropriation of Him as Saviour through faith.

The work of Christ Jesus in salvation is described in the words, "who abolished death, and brought life and immortality to light." The redemptive work of Christ is set forth under two aspects, the one destructive and the other constructive. "The two necessarily stand in contrast, yet not without a close and inward connection; for the one is but the reverse side of the other" (Fairbairn). He "abolished death," the death brought in by human sin, death in the fullest sense of the term. The word rendered "abolished" does not carry the thought of annihilation, but rather means to make of none effect, reduce to powerlessness. Death has not yet been abolished, but for the believer death has been deprived of its power and terrors.

by the removal of its sting. It has now become the gateway into the presence of God for the believer. The ultimate destruction of death is still future (I Cor. 15:26), but the aorist tense here points to the historic fact that Christ has rendered death of none effect through His own death and resurrection.

The further result of Christ's redemptive work was that He "brought life and immortality to light." His redemptive work "brought to light," lighted up, illuminated as the blazing light of the noonday sun, that which previously existed but was shrouded in uncertainty. The hope of immortality was in the world before but He brought it into a certainty through His teaching and above all by His own resurrection. The true meaning of "life," life in the highest sense, is seen only in Christ the glorified God-man. And this life is characterized by "immortality," better "incorruption, imperishability." The thought is that this life, in its full scope, applies also to our bodies, for corruption and decay pertain to our mortal bodies, not the soul. His own resurrection body brought this into view for the first time. The added words "through the gospel" remind us that this revelation is now made to us through the Gospel. Only comparatively few among the masses of humanity saw personally the manifestation of life and immortality in Christ; so it is through the preaching of the Gospel, in which this manifestation is enshrined, that this revelation is now made known to men.

b) The position and attitude of the apostle, vv. 11, 12. In typical Pauline fashion, the mention of the Gospel at once leads to a statement of his relation to that Gospel. As a second incentive to courage, he mentions his position in relation to the Gospel (v. 11) and indicates his attitude in suffering for it (v. 12).

i) His position in relation to the Gospel, v. 11. "Whereunto I was appointed a preacher, and an apostle, and a teacher." These three nouns set forth the nature of his office. The Greek word for "preacher" is "herald" and means one who makes a public announcement as ordered by another. It speaks of his appointment as a messenger to proclaim the Gospel message. "Apostle" points to the authority of the messenger, while "teacher" has reference to the method of imparting the message. The first term views his office in relation to his message, the second in relation to his credentials, the third in relation to those to whom he ministers.

ii) His attitude in suffering for the Gospel, v. 12. "For which cause," because of his relation to the Gospel as just enumerated, "I suffer also these things." He does not enumerate "these things," the harsh imprisonment as a malefactor, the abandonment, the unjust doom, the awful loneliness. They were well known to Timothy, hence need not be restated further to wrench the heart of Timothy. He is suffering, "yet I am not ashamed." He can testify personally to that which he has asked of Timothy (v. 8). And the secret of his attitude is a Person. "For I know him whom I have believed." It is his abiding knowledge of this Person that removes all sense of shame. The world may regard his faith in a crucified Jesus a thing of folly and a just cause for shame, but his personal relations with this Person prevent any such feeling. This Person will never put him to shame. He has permanently put his trust and confidence in Him (perfect tense), has been trusting Him all along, and is trusting Him now in the face of impending death. It is his settled, fixed assurance "that he is able to guard that which I have committed to him." The Greek is literally, "that he is able to guard my deposit." He has unshaken confidence in His ability to do what he trusts Him to do. He is able

42

effectively "to guard my deposit." The "deposit" may mean either what Paul has committed to God or what God has committed to him. The former view, given in our versions, regards the deposit variously as Paul's soul, his salvation, or his final reward. Thus viewed, God is pictured as the Trustee with whom he has deposited for safekeeping his temporal and eternal welfare. This truth provides wondrous comfort to the tried and tested servant of the Lord.

The majority of the Greek expositors, and many interpreters since, have held that the "deposit" is best explained here, as in the other passages where it occurs in the New Testament, in the sense of the Christian message with which Paul himself has been entrusted. The word occurs only in I Timothy 6:20, here, and in verse 14 following. In the other two passages the word clearly expresses what is committed by God to a person and for which he is answerable to God. This fact makes it probable that Paul, in the absence of any indication otherwise, uses it in the same sense here. (The pronoun "my" is indecisive and may be used with either connotation.) Thus viewed the meaning is that the precious deposit of the Gospel, which God has entrusted to Paul, God will not in these difficult times allow to be lost. In view of his impending martyrdom and the devastating persecutions of the Church which appear inevitable, Paul is confident that the all-powerful Guardian and Protector, whom he has learned to trust implicitly, will Himself safeguard the message which He has given. We let "the deposit" mean the Gospel which has been entrusted to him, yet this assurance ultimately includes himself, his all, since the preaching of that Gospel was his very life. His labors in the proclamation and defense of that message lead him to think of the day of future reward.

"Against that day" looks forward to that future day when Paul will stand before the judgment seat of Christ to receive his reward for his Gospel labors.

c. The fidelity of the minister, vv. 13-18. The third essential quality of the steadfast minister is fidelity to the truth of the Gospel. Paul makes a double appeal for steadfast loyalty to the Gospel (vv. 13, 14) and again appends an incentive to fidelity (vv. 15-18).

1) The appeal for fidelity, vv. 13, 14. Timothy is given a double exhortation. He is to hold the pattern of sound words (v. 13) and to guard the good deposit (v. 14).

a) The exhortation to hold the pattern of sound words, v. 13. Timothy is urged to continue to "hold," as he has faithfully been doing, "the pattern of sound words." The word "pattern," emphatic by position, means an outline, a sketch, a model. As an artist has his sketch before him, so Timothy is to use the outline which he has heard from Paul as his model for his work and never depart from it. And this is important because Paul's teaching consisted of "sound words." The word "sound" is literally "healthful," standing in sharp contrast to the sickly, impractical, and disease-producing teaching of the false teachers. This need for retaining and transmitting "sound" doctrine is stressed especially in this epistle.

Paul's reference to "the pattern of sound words" does not imply a fixed creedal formula to which Timothy is bound to adhere. It refers rather to the system of truth conveyed in divinely taught expressions which Timothy has heard from Paul. "From me" is emphatic by position as indicating the source from which Timothy has gained his knowledge of these truths. The reference to Paul's teaching under the word "pattern" implies that "such an outline may be expanded and that other statements of the truth will be helpful, but they must be in accordance with the beliefs which Paul himself has set forth in the gospel message committed to Timothy" (Erdman). The validity of a minister's message lies in its adherence to the great verities of the Christian revelation. Lipscomb remarks:

> None can be too careful in stating the truths of the Scriptures in the language of the inspired writers. When men cannot convey their thoughts in the words of the Scriptures, it is generally because they do not hold sound doctrine.

The spirit in which one clings to the truth is of vital importance. It is not to be a formal, lifeless retention of formulas. Hence Paul adds that Timothy is to do so "in faith and love which is in Christ Jesus." "In faith and love" mark the sphere in which the pattern of sound words must be held. "His theology is to be the theology of the heart, vitalized and spiritualized in the atmosphere of Christian faith and love" (Harvey). Timothy's faith is to be centered in God and His redemptive revelation, while his love, intelligent and purposeful, directs him in his work of teaching and guiding others. True love will not be indifferent to the promulgation of doctrine which is unhealthy and death-producing.

b) The exhortation to guard the good deposit, v. 14. "That good thing which was committed unto thee guard." "That good thing" is literally "the good deposit" and indicates the Gospel message committed to Timothy. The exhortation is parallel to the one in the previous verse. "The good deposit," like "pattern" in verse 13, stands in the place of emphasis; they are essentially the same. The healthful teaching becomes the deposit which he is urged effectively to "guard." That same Gospel which was committed to Paul has also been committed to Timothy and he must give diligence to guard it against loss or admixture with error by any heresy which seeks to pervert the Gospel.

In verse 12 Paul looked to God for the preservation of the deposit, while here he lays the duty upon Timothy. God's preservation of His truth does not relieve us of our responsibility to guard it. But Timothy is to do so, not in his own strength or watchfulness, but "through the Holy Spirit which dwelleth in us." The ministry of the Holy Spirit, who indwells all believers, will enable him to be a good custodian of the truth of the Gospel. "Then, as now, men who were wise in their own conceit, who trusted more to their own strength than to the guidance of the Holy Spirit, were preaching doctrines far removed from the teachings of Christ and his apostles" (Boise).

2) The incentive to fidelity, vv. 15-18. The presentation of personal examples is often an important stimulus for the diligent fulfillment of personal duty. Paul appeals to the power of human example, both negative and positive, as an incentive to Timothy for fidelity. He reminds him of the negative example of the Asiatics (v. 15) and holds up the positive example of Onesiphorus (vv. 16-18).

a) Neg.—the example of those in Asia, v. 15. By saying "this thou knowest," Paul indicates Timothy's personal awareness of this negative example. What might have been simply a cause for further depression to Timothy, Paul here turns into a constructive force. It is to be an incentive to him not to act like them. The solemn fact is that "all that are in Asia turned away from me." Those thus referred to were in "Asia," the Roman governmental province of Asia, at the time of writing. Being located in Asia, Timothy knew the facts. The expression "turned away" might imply doctrinal defection, but since they are introduced in contrast to the personal kindnesses of

Onesiphorus, the term does not necessarily mean more than standing aloof from him. "When they should have showed friendship, they ignored him" (Fairbairn). It would seem that Paul had written to Ephesus asking that some of his old acquaintances, men thoroughly familiar with his work and teaching, should come to Rome to testify in his behalf. But the apparent hopelessness of Paul's position and their fear of the possible consequences to themselves, had caused all of them to disregard the appeal. Men like Titus, Luke, or Timothy could not be called upon to testify in his behalf because they had aided and abetted him in the alleged crime. Among those who had thus turned away, Paul for some reason not stated mentions "Phygelus and Hermogenes." Nothing further is known about them. It is solemn to contemplate how their timidity and selfish fears have branded their names with an unsavory immortality. "It has been their destiny to be handed down to posterity as men who acted an unworthy part toward the most noble man of all time in his extremity" (Lipscomb and Shepherd).

b) Pos.—the courageous example of Onesiphorus, vv. 16-18. In contrast to the men just mentioned, Paul holds up the worthy example of another Ephesian, Onesiphorus. He utters a prayer for the house of Onesiphorus (v. 16a), pictures the services of Onesiphorus at Rome (vv. 16b, 17), breathes a prayer for Onesiphorus himself (v. 18a), and reminds Timothy of the man's previous ministries at Ephesus (v. 18b).

i) The prayer for the house of Onesiphorus, v. 16a. "The Lord grant mercy to the house of Onesiphorus." His grateful remembrance of the noble conduct of Onesiphorus causes Paul to breathe a prayer for his family. The family evidently lived at Ephesus since Paul sends greetings to them through Timothy (4:19). Onesiphorus, whose name means "help-bringer," had lived up to the meaning of his name. Thus to render his services to Paul the prisoner entailed expense, effort, and personal risk, and the entire family of Onesiphorus shared the cost. The following "for" shows that Paul recognized this and in consequence petitions the divine mercy upon them.

ii) The services of Onesiphorus at Rome, vv. 16b, 17. With graphic strokes Paul paints the picture of the services of Onesiphorus at Rome. He reverses the order of events, listing them not in the order of actual occurrence, but in the order in which he learned of them. "He oft refreshed me," Paul gratefully records. The word means "to cool again, to cool off." The repeated comfort received from him caused Paul to breathe more easily in his dark dungeon. These ministries were so refreshing to Paul because they proved that he "was not ashamed of my chain." Others have shown that they were ashamed, but not so noble Onesiphorus. The mention of his "chain" (singular) reminds us that Paul was chained to a soldier.

Instead of being ashamed of Paul, Onesiphorus, when he came to Rome, "sought me diligently, and found me." The fact that it required diligent and persistent search to find Paul shows that this is a different imprisonment than that of Acts 28, when Paul lived in his own hired house and all were free to come to him. Now he is kept in close confinement and is difficult to locate. Tradition has located this imprisonment in the "Well-Dungeon" at the foot of the Capitol, a damp and chilly vaulted pit. To find him there showed that Onesiphorus sought "diligently." (The rendering "very diligently" in the King James is based on the comparative form of the adverb found in some old manuscripts.) "And found me" sounds like an exclamation. What a glad surprise it was for Paul to be found there by this loyal friend!

iii) The prayer for Onesiphorus, v. 18a. His gratitude and love cause Paul to breathe a prayer for Onesiphorus personally. "The Lord grant unto him to find mercy of the Lord in that day." The repetition of the word "Lord" is striking. Seemingly it is due to the surge of Paul's thoughts. "The Lord grant" had apparently already become a formula of invocation, hence the repetition of the word would come naturally as he thinks of the Person being petitioned to grant the desired mercy. The kindness of Onesiphorus, which the aged apostle now facing martyrdom will never be able to repay, he desires the Lord to repay "in that day," that is, the future day of judgment. The prayer thus does not relate to the time between death and resurrection but looks forward to the time of the return of Christ. It has often been concluded from these verses that Onesiphorus was dead at the time of writing. But this assumption is gratuitous. Unquestionably Paul does at times ask eschatological blessings for those who, while he is writing, are still living on earth (cf. I Thess. 5:23, 24); hence his prayer for Onesiphorus here does not prove that he has died. Nor does the mention of "the house" of Onesiphorus (v. 16) imply his death. In I Corinthians 16:15 Paul speaks of the "house" of a certain man who certainly was alive at the time of writing. Paul has breathed a prayer for the "house of Onesiphorus," not because the head of the house was dead, but because the whole family had shared in the highly appreciated ministries which he has rendered. At any rate, this passage cannot be used to support the unscriptural practice of praying for the dead. And even if he has actually died, the prayer does not ask for his deliverance from purgatory but that he may find mercy in the final day of judgment.

iv) The ministry of Onesiphorus at Ephesus, v. 18b.

What Onesiphorus has done at Rome is only an instance in a life marked with kindly ministries to others. Hence Paul goes back to his previous experiences with Onesiphorus. "In how many things he ministered at Ephesus, thou knowest very well." (The insertion of the words "unto me" in the King James Version rests on insufficient manuscript evidence.) These ministries at Ephesus were not limited to Paul; they were rendered to the whole church. The word "ministered" is used in a technical sense at times to denote the service of deacons, but the use of the word here does not prove that Onesiphorus was an official deacon. They were not official services rendered in fulfillment of his office, but they were love-prompted deeds of Christian kindness. Of these ministries "thou [emphatic pronoun] knowest very well." The verb "knowest" points to Timothy's experiential knowledge of them. He realized them "very well," literally "better," that is, better than Paul could describe them.

2. *The Duties of the Steadfast Minister*, 2:1-13

Thou therefore, my child, be strengthened in the grace that is in Christ Jesus. And the things which thou hast heard from me among many witnesses, the same commit thou to faithful men, who shall be able to teach others also. Suffer hardship with me, as a good soldier of Christ Jesus. No soldier on service entangleth himself in the affairs of this life; that he may please him who enrolled him as a soldier. And if also a man contend in the games, he is not crowned, except he have contended lawfully. The husbandman that laboreth must be the first to partake of the fruits. Consider what I say; for the Lord shall give thee understanding in all things. Remember Jesus Christ, risen from the dead, of the seed of David, according to my gospel: wherein I suffer hardship unto bonds, as a malefactor; but the word of God is not bound. Therefore I endure all things for the elect's sake, that they also may obtain the salvation which is in Christ Jesus with eternal glory. Faithful is the saying: For if we died with him, we shall also live with him: if we endure, we shall also reign with him: if we shall deny him, he also will deny us: if we are faithless, he abideth faithful; for he cannot deny himself.

With the opening words, "thou therefore, my child," Paul again turns to Timothy with further exhortations. The "thou" is emphatic, clearly marking a direct appeal to Timothy, while the tender address "my child" reminds him that what is now to be urged upon him comes from the tender, yearning heart of his spiritual father. "Therefore" connects these duties with what has gone before. Some interpreters hold that the connection is with the mention of the sad defection in 1:15 and the contrasting noble example of Onesiphorus. It seems better to regard the connection as being with all that Paul has appealed for in chapter 1. The duties now urged naturally follow out of the thought of the essential qualities of the steadfast minister just presented. Paul now sets before Timothy the duties of personal strengthening (v. 1), of transmitting the truth (v. 2), and of steadfastly enduring for the Gospel (vv. 3-13).

a. The duty of personal strengthening, v. 1. "Be strengthened in the grace that is in Christ Jesus." It is not an appeal for him to summon up and assert his own strength. He is not asked to "be strong" but "be strengthened," to be made strong. The present tense denotes the continuing experience, thus "expressing a continuous and growing consolidation of character" (Pope). He is to let the Lord fill him with strength. Although the verb is passive, this experience of being made strong involves the co-operation of the one being strengthened. The believer is not just a passive recipient of this strength; he must actively appropriate the source of strength lying in God's "grace." This is grace in the fullest sense, "given us in Christ Jesus before times eternal" (1:9). It is here designated as the grace "that is in Christ Jesus." This grace is embodied in Christ Jesus who imparts it to all who are in living union with Him, just as the vine imparts its life and fruitfulness to the branches that are in abiding union with it.

b. The duty of transmitting the truth, v. 2. "And" links this duty with the previous duty of personal strengthening, but logically follows it. The personal experience of being made strong in grace qualifies him to transmit the precious deposit of the Gospel to others. It is also true that transmitting to others the truths which have embedded themselves in our own hearts and lives constitutes a means of personal strengthening. He is to transmit "the things which thou hast heard from me." Some scholars hold that the verb "heard" (aorist tense) points to the time of Timothy's ordination when Paul set forth the basic truths of the Gospel before him. But it is quite unnecessary thus to limit the reference. The aorist tense rather sums up as a historic fact the varied occasions when Timothy has heard Paul present these Gospel truths (cf. 1:13) "among many witnesses" (2:2). The word translated "among" (*dia*) here does not denote the agents through whom Timothy heard them but means "in the presence of," and is indicative of the nature of the things heard. They were not private communications, restricted to an inner group, but were heard by "many witnesses" who could testify to the truth of the things taught by Paul. There is not the slightest ground for holding that the apostles had any esoteric doctrines which were privately communicated to their successors. The reference is to the truths which have been preserved for us in the Pauline

Epistles. Those who would limit the reference to Timothy's ordination understand these "many witnesses" to mean the presbyters of the churches. On the other view the reference is much broader and refers to the believing multitudes, both Jew and Gentile, who, with Timothy, had at different times listened to Paul's preaching.

The things thus heard, constituting the "good deposit" of the Gospel (1:14, Gr.), Timothy is to "commit," to "deposit" with others. (The noun and the verb in the Greek have the same root.) They must be "faithful men," not only believers but reliable and trustworthy men, further described as men "who shall be able to teach others also." They must be able and competent in turn to pass on to others this treasure by their ability and willingness to teach. Paul received this treasure from the Lord and passed it on to Timothy, who is to pass it on to other capable men, who in turn will pass it on to others from generation to generation. Lenski well remarks:

> This is the true apostolic succession of the ministry, not an uninterrupted line of hands laid on, extending back to the apostles themselves, with all ordinations not in that line null and void; but a succession of true apostolic doctrine, the deposit of what we still hear from Paul in his writings, this held by us in faithful hearts, with competency to teach others these same things. The apostle evidently did not expect the future teachers of the Church to produce new or different teaching. The Gospel is changeless in all ages.

Here is the picture of Christianity being perpetuated through a successful teaching ministry, maintaining from age to age the apostolic principles of faith and practice. These teachers must teach "others also." The term "others" naturally includes the rising generation of ministers in the church but need not be restricted to ministers, since the entire congregation must be the recipient of this teaching.

c. The duty of steadfast endurance for the Gospel, vv. 3-13. This duty is basic in the purpose of this epistle and is set forth at considerable length. It is the main admonition and is introduced without a connecting formula. (The "thou therefore" in the King James Version is omitted in the most ancient manuscripts.) Paul presents the demand for endurance in the Christian life (vv. 3-7) and offers a threefold statement of motivation (vv. 8-13).

1) The demand for endurance in the Christian life, vv. 3-7. Paul opens with a direct appeal to Timothy to suffer hardship as a good soldier (v. 3), gives three brief pictures setting forth the demands of the Christian life (vv. 4-6), and closes with an appeal to understand the pictures (v. 7).

a) The call to suffer hardship as a good soldier, v. 3. "Suffer hardship with me." The verb, already used in 1:8, is a compound form meaning to suffer what is bad, to suffer ill treatment. The limiting pronoun "me" is not stated in the Greek, as shown by the use of italics, but is inferred from the preposition "with" in the original verb. "With me" limits the meaning too much; the Greek warrants only the general thought of sharing ill with his comrades, Paul as well as others, "take thy share in suffering." It reminds him that he is not alone in the battle, there are others who are enduring with him "as a good soldier of Christ Jesus." Paul's figure does not, of course, sanction the art of war, but was chosen aptly to set forth the rigorous demands of the Christian life. It is a common figure with the apostle (cf. I Cor. 9:7; II Cor. 10:3-6; Eph. 6:10-20). Timothy is urged to be a "good," that is a noble or excellent, soldier "of Christ Jesus," belonging to Him and engaged in warfare for Him.

b) The pictures of the Christian life, vv. 4-6. Just what is involved in being a "good soldier" Paul indicates by his illustrations of the soldier (v. 4), the athlete (v. 5), and the farmer (v. 6). The three pictures belong together and set forth the demands and rewards of the Christian life.

i) The picture of the soldier, v. 4. "No soldier on service" may more literally be rendered "no one soldiering," or "no soldier on active service," and presents the soldier as being on active duty, not on furlough or even in stationary quarters. As such he does not, and must not, "entangle himself in the affairs of this life." He must not become "entangled" or entwined in the business pursuits of civilian life whereby men ordinarily earn their living. He must keep habitually free from getting himself tied up in these pursuits so that he is not at liberty to devote himself to his primary duty. That does not mean that the Christian minister must never engage in "secular work" for a living, but rather "he is to avoid absorption in it, or complications in connection with it, such as may divert him in spirit from his higher, divine calling" (Harvey). Paul engaged in "tentmaking" for a living, but it was only a means toward his master passion of preaching the Gospel. Nor did the early Christian church understand this passage as forbidding a trade to the minister. Yet experience has amply shown that the minister can best fulfill his high calling when he is freed from the necessity of earning a living through secular labor and is enabled to devote his full time, strength, and thought to his office. (Cf. II Cor. 11:8-15.) As he thus gives himself fully to his calling, allowing no side-pursuits to interfere with his duties as Christ's soldier, he will be able to "please him who enrolled him as a soldier." His primary concern will ever be to win the commendation of God who enlisted him in

His army. This was Paul's constant ambition (II Cor. 5:9) and he now holds it up before Timothy. The paramount concern of every Christian should be to please the Lord in every area of his life.

ii) The picture of the athlete, v. 5. "And" adds this picture as an additional thought. He must also compete according to the rules to be rewarded. In saying "if also a man contend in the games" Paul draws his figure from the well-known athletic contests in the Grecian games. These games had captured the interests of all Greece and were as popular with the common people as baseball is in America. These games made strenuous demands upon those who participated. But Paul's thought here rather turns to the reward; the athlete "is not crowned, except he have contended lawfully." The crowning, the goal in all the effort put forth, could be won only if he had "contended lawfully," according to all the rules of the game, both for the preliminary training and the actual contest. No infringement of the rules was condoned. Even so the servant of the Lord is called to be as careful as an athlete in adhering to the rules of his calling, making the revealed will of God his guiding standard in all things. As Van Oosterzee remarks:

> The minister of the gospel dare not arbitrarily exempt himself from this or that portion of his task, or even direct his activity according to his own discretion; not the bias of his own heart, but the will of the Lord alone must be his standard; so that, without this, it is impossible for him to hope for His approval and recognition.

iii) The picture of the farmer, v. 6. This picture completes the thought of reward already implied in the reference to the crowning of the athlete. "The husbandman that laboreth must be the first to partake of the fruits." The picture deals with the tiller of the soil, "the hard-working farmer," as Moule aptly renders it. There is no intended contrast between the farmer that "laboreth" and the farmer who does not. Toiling lies in the very nature of his occupation. The farmer who does not toil does not produce fruit either for himself or for others. Paul's emphasis is rather that "it is necessary for the toiling farmer first to be partaking of the fruits" (lit. rendering). If the farmer does not first share in the fruits of his labors, does not realize a profit, his farming will soon come to an end. But the farmer produces his fruits not just for himself but for others. The fruits of the minister are produced through his preaching of the Gospel, producing fruit in the life of others. But in thus producing fruits in the lives of others he is the first to partake of the blessings of the Gospel. He has the reward already in this life of partaking year by year of the fruits of his labors, but he will reap the harvest of his labors in the glory beyond.

c) The duty to understand the pictures, v. 7. "Consider what I say." It is not that Timothy cannot grasp the meaning of the figures, but there is so much involved in them that he must be applying his mind to them to apprehend their full application. And Timothy need not fear that the mental activity demanded will be ineffectual. He is given the assurance that "the Lord shall give thee understanding in all things." (The reading in the King James Version, making it a prayer, is based on a reading less well attested.) He need not depend upon his own imperfect, erring mental faculties; for the needed enlightenment he is directed to the Lord. "Timothy was referred for insight and exposition not to the Church, not to the Apostle, or to the Apostles, but to the divine Master Himself, present, attentive, cognizant of Timothy's individual difficulties and mental needs" (Moule). The apprehension of spiritual truth is not primarily a matter of mental acumen but of spiritual teachableness.

2) The motivation for endurance in the Christian life, vv. 8-13. Having set forth the picture of the Christian life as one demanding the enduring of suffering, Paul next sets before Timothy three motivating forces undergirding such a life. He is to be motivated by the constant remembrance of Jesus Christ (v. 8), the example of Paul's own suffering (vv. 9, 10), and the certainty of future reward from the Lord (vv. 11-13).

a) The constant remembrance of Jesus Christ, v. 8. "Remember Jesus Christ." The present imperative points to the continuing duty, "Keep on remembering Jesus Christ." It is of utmost importance for steadfastness in suffering for our Lord. The vivid remembrance of Him and all that He is and has done keeps our relationship with Him vital and effective. If this is neglected it is quite possible for us as Christian workers amid the very stress and noise of religious work to forget Jesus Christ until we lose vital contact with Him and our lives become powerless and ineffective.

According to the critical text, this is the only place in II Timothy where Paul uses the order "Jesus Christ." (See on 1:1.) The order calls attention to the fact that the historical Jesus, who walked this earth and suffered opposition, and death, was in His resurrection revealed to be the Christ, the fulfillment of Messianic prophecy.

Timothy is to continue remembering Jesus Christ in a twofold way, as "risen from the dead, of the seed of David." The perfect tense of the participle rendered "risen" denotes not merely the fact of His resurrection but that He is now the ever-living risen Lord. The human Jesus who once suffered and died is no longer in the tomb, but is alive forevermore and able to aid and sustain

Timothy, and every afflicted believer. Not the vision of a crucified Jesus but the vision of a risen Lord is held up before Timothy. He is to remember the victorious, living Lord. He is further described as "of the seed of David." The expression does point to the fact of His human nature but goes far beyond that. Being "the seed of David" He has the Messianic qualifications and is the Heir of all the glorious promises of God to David concerning the throne and kingdom of his Son. As such, He is the reigning one; He is now seated in glory on His Father's throne (Rev. 3:21) and will come again to reign over this world.

This concept of Jesus Christ, Paul reminds Timothy, is "according to my gospel." It is in full accord or harmony with the Gospel which had been entrusted to Paul and which he ceaselessly proclaimed.

b) The suffering of Paul in the Gospel, vv. 9, 10. Paul's reference to his Gospel at once calls forth a statement of his relation to that Gospel, "wherein I suffer hardship unto bonds." His present suffering in prison is due to his relation to the Gospel which he preaches. It is the sphere "wherein" his suffering of ill treatment occurs, and that even "unto bonds, as a malefactor." The word "malefactor" occurs elsewhere in the New Testament only in Luke 23, where it is applied to the crucified robbers, and indicates that he is suffering "the utmost shame and disgrace as a criminal of the most shameful and disgraceful kind" (Lenski). Paul's sensitive nature was keenly conscious of the indignities being heaped upon him because of his relation to the Gospel. The word indicates that Paul's second imprisonment must have been harsh indeed and stands in striking contrast to the lenient treatment received during his first imprisonment (Acts 28:30, 31).

Yet amid such suffering Paul exults in the realization

that "the word of God is not bound." "The word of God" designates the Gospel from the side of its divine origin. The messenger of that word may be "bound" but the message itself cannot be fettered. All the prisons and chains of Christ-defying rulers cannot imprison its progress. Harvey comments:

> With irresistible, divine energy it is advancing in its career of triumph, even while its defenders suffer imprisonment and martyrdom. Men die, but Christ and His gospel live and triumph through the ages.

"Therefore," because the Word of God remains unimprisoned, Paul courageously continues, "I endure all things for the elect's sake." He continues to "endure" with brave, willing persistency to bear up under the load of persecution being heaped upon him, and he does so "for the elect's sake." Although the sufferings are keenly felt, he willingly endures them for he recognizes that they have a moral and spiritual purpose. Through his sufferings the elect "obtain the salvation which is in Christ." "He was suffering for the elect in the very spirit of Christ; not indeed with a view to the blotting out of sin, which Christ alone could effect, but none the less with the aim of expediting their full experience of salvation and final entrance into glory" (Lilley). Since the elect are appointed to be saved "in sanctification . . . and belief of the truth" (II Thess. 2:13), and the preaching of the Gospel is therefore necessary for their obtaining of salvation, Paul gladly suffers in connection with his preaching that they may "also" be saved. Paul's "also" reminds us that he is not simply interested in his own salvation but in that of others as well. This salvation is described as that "which is in Christ Jesus with eternal glory." Salvation is possessed now by the believer, but Paul is thinking of the final consummation of that salvation at the return of

Christ with the resultant "eternal glory" for the saved. Since this is the purpose of God for the elect, Paul is willing to suffer that they may "obtain" this salvation. It must be obtained, for election does not eliminate or put any restrictions on the exercise of human freedom in meeting the conditions for salvation.

Paul bravely endured for the elect, and only eternity will reveal what that endurance has meant for the salvation of souls. Horton aptly comments:

> What would have happened if Paul had not endured? If he, like Demas, had proved traitor to the gospel, humanly speaking the elect would not have heard the good news, and the stream of truth would have been dammed up at its source.

The realization of the possible far-reaching consequences of his endurance is to stimulate Timothy to endure steadfastly as a good soldier of Christ Jesus. And does the realization of the possible impact of our influence and example nerve us to persevere amid difficulty in our own little sphere of service?

c) The certainty of the future reward, vv. 11-13. As a third motive for suffering for Christ's cause, Paul holds up the certainty of the relation between our conduct here and our future condition. It seems best, with our versions, to regard the opening words, "Faithful is the saying," as pointing to what follows. They are intended to emphasize them as containing truth of weighty significance and worthy of the fullest confidence. The formula is peculiar to the Pastoral Epistles (I Tim. 1:15; 3:1; 4:9; Titus 3:8; here). They seem to introduce the quotation of some pithy evangelical saying that had gained currency in the early church. It is generally held that the statements which follow are a quotation from an ancient Christian hymn. The rhythmical form of the statements lends credence to this view; they may be a part of one of the "spiritual songs" which Paul mentions elsewhere (Eph. 5:19; Col. 3:16), but it cannot be proved. Lilley contends that these words are "rather an outburst of the lyric spirit that filled the apostle's heart, attaining its present shape by ceaseless thought on the pervasive power of union with Christ and frequent repetition in preaching." Certainly their poetic character does not prove that Paul could not have written them.

The central truth of these pithy statements is that faith in Christ identifies the believer with Him in everything while unbelief just as surely separates men from Him. The four "if" clauses with their conclusions fall into two pairs, the first positive (11, 12a) and the second negative (12b, 13). The "if" does not imply any uncertainty or doubt but for purposes of presentation is regarded as fulfilled, as true; the inevitable conclusion then follows. We may set them forth as follows:

> If we died with him,
>> we shall also live with him:
> if we endure,
>> we shall also reign with him:
> if we shall deny him,
>> he also will deny us:
> if we are faithless,
>> he abideth faithful;
> for he cannot deny himself.

The first pair points to the results of enduring ill treatment for Christ. "If we died with him." The tense of the word "died" naturally points to a past fact. Commentators differ as to the reference. One view regards it as symbolically pointing to the rite of baptism, as in Romans 6:4, 8, when the believer was united with Christ in death as a spiritual reality. But the teaching in Romans 6 occurs in an entirely different context than the present passage.

The context here seems rather to point to physical death as the highest point of suffering for Christ. The reference is then to a martyr's death now viewed from the standpoint of the crowning day. It is the purpose of the passage to give encouragement to suffer for Christ even unto death. If loyalty to Christ for us means physical death, the assurance is that "we shall also live with him." Faithfulness to the point of the supreme sacrifice for Christ assures us of eternal fellowship with Him in resurrection glory.

Endurance for Him does not require a martyr's death of most believers, but continued endurance in daily life is required. "If we endure" points to this continuing experience of bravely bearing up under the hardships and afflictions heaped upon the believer because of his relation to Christ. The assurance is given that "we shall also reign with him." Those who share His rejection now are assured of sharing in His triumph when He comes to reign.

By contrast, the second pair asserts the solemn warning that denial and unfaithfulness just as surely separate men from Christ. "If we deny him" points to an awful possibility. Jesus Himself emphatically warned of the danger (Matt. 10:33; Mark 8:38). To close our eyes to this warning would be folly. William Kelly comments:

> There was danger in a day of declension particularly of departure not only from this or that divine principle but from Himself, and this permanently. Nor does the apostle bolster up the saints in what is the most dangerous delusion, that there is no danger. For dangers abound on all sides; and we ought to know that grievous times were to come in the last times.

To "deny him" here does not point merely to a temporary weakness of faith, as in the case of Peter (Luke 22:54-62), but as the conclusion shows, means to deny our relation with Him as a permanent fact. The inevitable result is that "he also will deny us."

The warning is repeated in the final sentence, "if we are faithless, he abideth faithful." To be "faithless" means to give up one's faith and the present tense denotes this as the habitual attitude, not a temporary lapse or obscuration of faith. But in contrast to human faithlessness, "he abideth faithful," faithful to His warning that the unbelieving will be rejected. "Christ will never depart from that solemn word, which pledges Him, at the last day, to own those who have owned Him, and to deny those who have denied Him" (Harvey). His unchanging faithfulness arises out of the fact of His immutable nature. This is confirmed by the concluding statement which amplifies all of the preceding statements and forms the capstone for the whole. "For he cannot deny himself." As the unchanging Jehovah whose very nature is truth, He cannot be false to His own nature, nor to His word of promise to the faithful and His word of threatening to the faithless.

II. THE EXHORTATIONS TO DOCTRINAL SOUNDNESS, 2:14—4:8

IN THE PRECEDING PART of the epistle Paul has been dealing with the personal qualifications of the minister and his duties as a steadfast minister. In the remainder of the epistle (2:14-4:8) Paul turns to exhortations to doctrinal soundness in view of the heresies appearing in the church. He sets forth the minister's reaction to doctrinal error (2:14-26), offers instruction concerning the coming apostasy (3:1-17), and concludes with a final appeal to Timothy (4:1-8).

1. *The Minister's Reaction to Doctrinal Error,* 2:14-26

Of these things put them in remembrance, charging them in the sight of the Lord, that they strive not about words, to no profit, to the subverting of them that hear. Give diligence to present thyself approved unto God, a workman that needeth not to be ashamed, handling aright the word of truth. But shun profane babblings: for they will proceed further in ungodliness, and their word will eat as doth a gangrene: of whom is Hymenaeus and Philetus; men who concerning the truth have erred, saying that the resurrection is past already, and overthrow the faith of some. Howbeit the firm foundation of God standeth, having this seal, The Lord knoweth them that are his: and, Let every one that nameth the name of the Lord depart from unrighteousness. Now in a great house there are not only vessels of gold and of silver, but also of wood and of earth; and some unto honor, and some unto dishonor. If a man therefore purge himself from these, he shall be a vessel unto honor, sanctified, meet for the master's use, prepared unto every good work. But flee youthful lusts, and follow after righteousness, faith, love, peace, with them that call on the Lord out of a pure heart. But foolish and ignorant questionings refuse, knowing that they gender strifes. And the Lord's servant must not strive, but be gentle toward all, apt to teach, forbearing, in meekness correcting them that oppose themselves; if peradventure God may give them repentance unto the knowledge of the truth, and they may recover themselves out of the snare of the devil, having been taken captive by him unto his will.

Painfully conscious of the rising doctrinal errors within the sphere of the professing church, Paul sets before Timothy the minister's urgent activity amid doctrinal error (vv. 14-19) and stresses the need for holiness of life amid such error (vv. 20-26).

a. The urgent activity amid doctrinal error, vv. 14-19. Paul indicates the necessary activity of the minister when confronted with error (vv. 14-16a) and points out the reasons for the activity (vv. 16b-19).

1) The nature of the activity, vv. 14-16a. As a good minister of Jesus Christ, Timothy must take an active stand against error by solemn warning against it (v. 14), by his own example as a master-workman (v. 15), and by a deliberate shunning of profane babblings (v. 16a).

a) His warning against doctrinal error, v. 14. By pressing upon Timothy the standing duty, "of these things put them in remembrance," Paul points out the prophylactic against error. "These things" may include all that has been said thus far, but the immediate reference is to the fundamental truths expressed in verses 11-13 above. A serious endeavor to realize the relative importance of time and eternity is an effective restraint upon futile word-battles, such as were occupying the thoughts and energies of certain ones at Ephesus. The "them" need not be restricted to the "faithful men" whom Timothy was to train (2:2) but properly includes all believers. By saying "put them in remembrance" he implies that these truths were known to the church but that they needed continued reminding of them.

But Timothy must also give a categorical warning against error. "Charging them in the sight of the Lord, that they strive not about words." The charge is to be delivered "in the sight of the Lord," in the consciousness of the Lord's presence—"a very earnest, solemn thought for every public teacher, and one calculated *now,* as *then,* to deepen the life of one appointed to such an office" (Spence). Timothy must continually warn them "that they strive not about words"; they must refrain from engaging in "word-battles," wordy controversies and quibbling about words. The reason for the warning is, negatively, that such word-battles are of "no profit," for they never lead to moral and spiritual edification; positively, they will always, however unintentionally, produce the opposite result, "subverting them that hear." The word "subverting" means turning upside down. From it comes our English word "catastrophe." Many a religious debate has been a real catastrophe, as church history amply confirms. Such debates increase rather than remove doubts and stir up the bitterest passions.

b) His example as a master-workman, v. 15. Timothy must use the influence of positive personal example. "Give diligence to present thyself approved unto God." The word rendered "study" in the King James Version does not refer to the minister's study of books or the Scriptures, nor to his sermon preparation. It means "to make haste, to exert oneself, to be zealous or eager, to give diligence," with the further thought of effort, as papyrus usage shows. Timothy must put forth diligent effort to present himself "approved unto God," as a servant presents himself before his master with the consciousness of having done his master's will. In his work as a minister Timothy's chief concern must be not to win the approval of men but of God. Where there is lacking conscious integrity before God there cannot be boldness in rebuking the evils of men. It must be his concern to appear before God "as one tested," hence one who is "approved unto God."

As one who is "approved unto God," Timothy must be "a workman that needeth not to be ashamed." He must be a "workman," not a quibbler about vain and unprofitable words. The term "workman" points not to the needed skill in the performance of his task but rather to the laboriousness involved in its accomplishment. To be an acceptable minister demands strenuous and exhausting toil. Before the judgment seat of Christ he will be found a workman that "needeth not to be ashamed," no offense bringing shame upon him because of God's disapproval.

Further, as an approved workman he must be characterized as one "handling aright the word of truth." The word rendered "handling aright" (*orthotomounta*) is capable of several interpretations, as the margin in the American Standard Version indicates. Literally the word means "cutting evenly, or in a straight line." The figure behind the word has been held to be that of cutting a furrow, or a mason cutting stones straight, or as derived from Paul's own tent-making. It may well be that in this compound verb the idea of "cutting" falls into the background and the word is used to signify "handling aright," administering it in a truthful way, as contrasted to striving about words. Thus the meaning "to manage rightly, to treat truthfully without falsifying" (Alford) suits the requirements of the context. That which he handles aright is "the word of truth," the truth of God's revelation in the Gospel as contrasted to the empty chatter of the Ephesian errorists. The approved minister presents the eternal truths of the Gospel with fidelity, presses them on the consciences of men, and refuses to resort to tortuous interpretations of God's Word. He recognizes the proper division of God's revelation and handles it accordingly.

c) His shunning of profane babblings, v. 16a. "But shun profane babblings." He must show his attitudes toward these unholy errors by "shunning" them, literally, going around so as to avoid them. The proper attitude toward them is contempt. These "profane babblings" are unholy, "empty discourses, having sound rather than substance, dealing with subjects which are trifling rather than serious and weighty" (Harvey). To seek to answer them would be to give them a greater importance than they deserve.

2) The reasons for the activity, vv. 16b-19. Timothy must be actively opposed to error because of the destructive effect of error (vv. 16b-18) as well as the demand of divine truth (v. 19).

a) Because of the destructive effect of error, vv. 16b-18. Paul vividly pictures the errorists as to their character and influence. "For they [that is, the errorists themselves] will proceed further in ungodliness." These teachers apparently called themselves "the progressives," claiming an advanced type of Christian teaching. Ironically Paul admits that they "proceed further," or are "progressing," but it is a progress in ungodliness. They are diligently "chopping forward," thus removing every obstacle to reach their goal. The use of the future tense "will proceed" implies that the full development of their ungodliness has not yet been reached. Scripture and human experience confirm that there is a close connection between grave doctrinal error and a lax and purely selfish life. The influence of these errorists is deadly. "Their word," standing in sharp contrast to the word of truth (v. 15), "will eat as doth a gangrene." The word rendered "eat" is quite literally "will have pasture," like cattle grazing in every direction. It is a vivid picture of the rapid diffusion of their teaching, which is described as "a gangrene." It is "an eating sore," defined by Hippocrates to be "the state of a tumour between inflammation and entire mortification" (Alford). Error is a diffusive poison which, unless effectively checked, spreads rapidly through the whole body and leads to sure destruction.

Two examples of these errorists and their teaching are cited. "Of whom is Hymenaeus," perhaps the same man mentioned in I Timothy 1:20, "and Philetus." Of Philetus nothing further is known. If Hymenaeus is the same man whom Paul excommunicated, then the excommunication did not produce the result Paul had hoped for; he had persisted in his error. At any rate, these errorists continue to be professed Christians.

Their doctrinal perversity is pointed out when Paul describes them as "men who concerning the truth have erred." The truth from which they "have erred," literally, "missed the mark," is not a minor difference of opinion among men who were in basic agreement. It was a fundamental error, for they were "saying that the resurrection is past already." This was their "gangrene." They denied a future bodily resurrection and taught that the only resurrection there was had already occurred in the spiritual renewal of the believer in regeneration. They probably misapplied and allegorized Paul's teaching about the believer's spiritual union with Christ in death and resurrection, and insisted that the doctrine of the resurrection had only a spiritual meaning and application. "They allegorized away the doctrine, and turned all into figure and metaphor" (Waterland, quoted in Ellicott). Accepting the current philosophy that matter is evil, they argued that a physical resurrection was unthinkable.

The result of their teaching is that they "overthrow the faith of some." Their denial of the future resurrection was a subversion of the very fabric of "the faith." In I Corinthians 15 Paul shows that the doctrine of the bodily resurrection lies at the very foundation of the Christian faith. Hence the danger in their teaching. As Spence remarks:

In attacking, with their thinly veiled scepticism, the great doctrine of the resurrection of the body, in pushing aside the glorious hope, they touched with their impious

70

hands the cornerstone of all Christian belief—the resurrection in the body of the Redeemer.

By robbing certain ones of the hope of the resurrection they "overthrow," literally "turn upside down," the faith of "some." Apparently not many had as yet been infected with this gangrene, but if left unchecked its results would be fatal to the church. Even today the rationalists and modernists, while avoiding an open assertion that they do not believe in the resurrection, subvert the Biblical teaching by declaring that the spirit of Jesus, rather than His body, arose from the dead. Thus they subvert the historic faith. Instead of fellowshiping with such men as Christians, we had better classify them aright. They belong with Hymenaeus and Philetus.

b) Because of the demand of divine truth, v. 19. God demands separation from unrighteousness of His own, as Paul at once points out. The mention of the subversion of the faith of some does not mean that God's true Church can be destroyed. "Howbeit [or nevertheless] the firm foundation of God standeth." The cause of truth rests upon God's "firm foundation" which continues to stand in spite of the attacks of error and unbelief. The foundation is described as "firm" or "solid" in its nature, hence permanent and stable. The significance of the foundation has been variously interpreted. The context points to the meaning of the foundation as the whole body of genuine believers, the true Church of God built upon the apostolic doctrine.

Paul pictures God's firm foundation as having a two-fold "seal." The figure is not that of an "inscription" on a building, although many scholars advocate this picture. The seal was used to indicate ownership, security, and authenticity. Here the seal with its two legends speaks of ownership, security, and authenticity, certifying the genu-

71

ineness of those thus sealed. The seal with which believers are sealed indicates divine ownership, proclaims their security, and guarantees their genuineness.

This seal has two complementary readings: "The Lord knoweth them that are his: and, Let every one that nameth the name of the Lord depart from unrighteousness." To be valid, the two legends on the seal cannot be separated. The first emphasizes the objective fact of God's superintending knowledge of His own; the second stresses the need for man's holiness. The first is dated in eternity past; the second regulates the believer's present conduct. The first assures the security of the Church; the second requires its purity. The first is a truth to be believed; the second is a demand to be obeyed.

"The Lord knoweth them that are his." The verb is literally "knew," and the aorist tense takes us back into eternity when this seal was affixed once for all with present historical validity. By virtue of His sovereign grace, He foreknew them as His own. But the security of those thus known by God is not an arbitrary or mechanical matter. To those divinely sealed as known by God the second part of the seal also applies. To name "the name of the Lord" is to make a profession of belief in His claims, to acknowledge oneself as a believer. Of such God demands that they "depart from unrighteousness." The second legend is not merely an appended admonition or warning; it is an integral part of the seal. True trust in God for security must reveal itself in a life of effective separation from unrighteousness. This is God's demand upon and the characteristic of those who constitute the foundation of God.

b. The needed holiness of life amid doctrinal error, vv. 20-26. Although Timothy may be assured that the true Church of God will never be overthrown by the errone-

72

ous teachings of men, he must realize the fact of the presence of true and false believers in the professing church. This fact places upon the minister the need for separation from error and the practice of personal holiness in life. By the use of a figure Paul pictures the mixed condition in the professing church (vv. 20, 21) and then makes the application to the minister's work (vv. 22-26).

1) The picture of the mixed condition in the "great house," vv. 20, 21. Obviously Hymenaeus and Philetus were professed Christians, within the sphere of professing Christendom. Their presence would naturally raise the question for Timothy and others, if the firm foundation of God stands and the sealed are known by God and depart from evil, how are we to account for the presence in the church of such men as these, who do not depart from evil? Paul accordingly proceeds to show what the visible, professing church has become. He compares it to a "great house," the palace of a rich man, in which there are a variety of "vessels," namely, all the members who are counted as belonging to the Church. When viewed in its true inner relation to the Lord, the Church was pictured as "God's foundation." But viewed in its outward, visible, historical development, it has become "a great house" with its many vessels of mixed value and destiny. The thought turns to the different kinds of utensils found in the house. In his picture Paul presents the two types of utensils in the house (v. 20) and points out the consequent need for separation for a position of honor (v. 21).

a) The two types of utensils in the house, v. 20. In the great house of professing Christendom there are two general classes of vessels, but with variations in each class. From the standpoint of their value, there are "vessels of gold and silver," those that are prized and kept and not thrown away, representing the true Christians;

73

there are also vessels "of wood and of earth," those taken to the junk yard when they have served their purpose, representing false believers. From the standpoint of their destiny, there are vessels "unto honor," believers destined for honor, and some "unto dishonor," the fate of the unsaved. As professed Christians, all are in "a great house," and all are used by the divine owner to serve His own sovereign purpose. "Each of these classes, the true and the false, are consciously or unconsciously, willingly or unwillingly, serving the purposes of God and doing his work, but with a service dissimilar in its nature and with a different destined end" (Harvey).

b) The needed separation for a position of honor, v. 21. Such has become the condition of Christendom that one can no longer be assured that all who compose the visible church are truly regenerated and members of the Body of Christ. A mixed condition has developed. This of course does not mean that we are knowingly to tolerate the presence of unsaved members in our churches. But in many places the moral sensibility has fallen so low that the mass refuses to purge out the old leaven of evil doctrine and practice. The vessels "unto dishonor" have influence enough to remain in or often even control the assembly. Then it becomes the duty of the true believer to "purge himself from these," that is, the vessels unto dishonor.

In making the application in verse 21 Paul goes beyond the figure of vessels, for an inanimate vessel cannot adequately represent the fact of human responsibility. Since man has the power of choice, he can do something to prepare himself for a service unto honor. The condition is that he will "purge himself," or "cleanse himself" by effectively separating himself from these heretical teachers and their doctrines, thus avoiding defilement. The wording of the original expresses the thoroughness of the separation from the corrupting environment of evil company. The reference is not merely to an inner moral separation but also to an outward separation. Involved is the obligation to refuse to fellowship with such enemies of the fundamentals of the faith. But as Kelly aptly observes:

> It may be noticed that there is no such thought as quitting the house, though some have fallen into this misconception in their zeal for holiness. . . Purging oneself from evil-doers within the house is not to leave the house, but to walk there as one ought according to scripture. . . Christendom is not given up by walking more according to God's will in the true path for Christians, whether individually or corporately.

Such purging of himself is necessary to be "a vessel unto honor." Such a vessel is further described by two perfect participles which indicate lasting conditions, and between them a descriptive adjective: (1) "sanctified," permanently separated from evil and consecrated unto the Lord; (2) "meet for the master's use," that is, "easy to make use of, usable, well serviceable for the Master." The word "master" is *despotēs* and means one who has undisputed ownership and control; it speaks of our sovereign Lord who has final ownership of and alone determines the use of His vessels. (3) Such a one will be a vessel "prepared unto every good work," permanently prepared and equipped for all varieties of Christian service. Brown well summarizes the teaching:

> The Christian's goal is *honour,* the honour conferred by God; his principle is *holiness;* his aim is *service,* usefulness to his Master Christ: his watchword is *'be prepared,'* hold thyself ready at every moment for every sort of kind and charitable action.

2) The application to the minister's work, vv. 22-26.

In applying the picture to the work of Timothy, Paul urges a life of personal purity (v. 22), advises him to disdain foolish and ignorant questions (v. 23), and gives directions for dealing with those in error (vv. 24-26).

a) **The exhortation to personal purity of life, v. 22.** Timothy must avoid not only defilement from without (v. 21) but also defilement from within. The way to a life of personal purity is both negative and positive. He must continually "flee youthful lusts," any and every sinful yearning or craving to which the soul of a young or a comparatively young man is exposed. The reference to "youthful lusts" must not be limited to sexual desires, nor must they be excluded. Youth also has other temptations. "Pride, prejudice, ambition, anger, may check a young man's usefulness as really though not so manifestly as gross self-indulgence" (Lilley). "But," on the positive side, he must actively "follow after," pursue like a hunter pursues his game, definite Christian virtues, namely, "righteousness, faith, love, peace." "Righteousness" is moral rectitude in character and conduct; "faith" points to sincere and dynamic confidence in God; "love" speaks of deep affection which intelligently apprehends and yet loves; "peace" denotes that undisturbed harmony with true Christians which is not broken by strife and word-battles. "In short," says Fairbairn, "maintain a character such as becomes the gospel of Christ, adorned with the graces and virtues which it especially inculcates."

In pursuing these virtues Timothy will join company "with them that call on the Lord out of a pure heart." Here is Paul's description of those whom Timothy will know to be true brethren. They are characterized as calling "on the Lord" in faith and in worship, and that "out of a pure heart." "The source of all true and acceptable adoration is 'a pure heart,' that is, a heart in which insincerity has no place" (Pope).

b) The command to disdain foolish and ignorant questions, v. 23. "But foolish and ignorant questionings refuse." He is to "refuse," disdain to be bothered with questionings which are characterized as "foolish and ignorant." They are "foolish," silly and senseless, and "ignorant," or uninstructed, showing that the questioner has not been properly instructed in God's redemptive truth. The reference is to the heretical teachers who wished to argue their senseless and useless inquiries concerning genealogies and Jewish traditions (cf. I Tim. 1:4; 4:7). Timothy is not to bother trying to answer them, knowing their effect, "that they gender strifes." While serving no useful end, such questions give birth to heated controversy and arouse bitter enmities. This however does not mean that all controversy with error is to be refused. As Brown remarks:

> It would be difficult to exaggerate the debt we owe to the great champions of the Christian Faith, who by word and pen and life prevented the Church from being led away by the plausible inventions of heretics. . . But controversy, if it is to justify itself, must (1) be occupied with questions which have a real bearing on faith and morals, and (2) must be conducted without loss of the peaceful temper.

c) The directions for dealing with those in error, vv. 24-26. Paul reminds Timothy of the demeanor necessary in dealing with those in error (vv. 24, 25a), as well as the aim in dealing with them (vv. 25b, 26).

i) The demeanor of the one dealing with them, vv. 24, 25a. This is presented both negatively and positively. Negatively, "the Lord's servant must not strive." Instead of continuing in the second person, Paul now uses the third person, thus including himself and any other man who holds a position as "the Lord's servant." As the Lord's "bondservant," carrying out his Master's will, he must not yield to the temptation to engage in worthless controversy with others. "But," on the contrary, he must be characterized by a very different demeanor, which is is given a fourfold description. First, he must be "gentle toward all," the opposite of harsh and irritable. He must be mild, benevolent, and approachable "to all," even those who are antagonistic to him. Second, he must be "apt to teach." He must possess not only the ability but also that readiness which leads him to impart counsel and instruction as opportunity arises. The third requirement is that he be "forbearing." His gentleness will not always be reciprocated but will be met with hostile scorn and ridicule; then he must be "forbearing," patient under injuries, putting up with the evil without loss of temper. The final requirement is, "in meekness correcting them that oppose themselves." The false teachers and those led astray by them may "oppose themselves" and reveal their hostility, but they are to be met with "meekness," without pride or an air of superiority, while he aims at "correcting them." The word rendered "correcting" is literally "child training," and implies instruction, correction, and discipline. In meekness he must instruct the uninstructed, correct the erring, and discipline the undisciplined. For this difficult task a spirit of meekness is indispensable.

ii) The aim in dealing with them, vv. 25b, 26. Paul clearly sets forth the aim in such pastoral work. "If peradventure God may give them repentance unto the knowledge of the truth." This hope for their repentance is stated hesitatingly—"if peradventure"—not because God is unwilling to give them repentance but because the habit of the errorists to contradict the truth has made it hard for them even to listen to the truth. Only God can effect the change in them. He must "give" it to them as a gift, using Timothy's efforts as the means to work the needed "repentance" in them. What they need is a definite change of heart and will. Their doctrinal perversions rooted in a moral perversity. Vital religious error has its roots in sin, and its removal demands not merely a change of mind but a change in the moral nature as well. The needed repentance is "unto the knowledge of the truth," the full apprehension and realization of (the) truth. "Only through a change in the moral disposition do men attain to the full knowledge, the believing apprehension, of the Gospel" (Harvey).

The hoped-for result of such work with the errorists is further described from the standpoint of the liberating effect of God's gift of repentance to them. The hope is that "they may recover themselves out of the snare of the devil." The word "recover" means literally "to return to soberness." The snare of the Devil into which they have fallen was the error by which they have become intoxicated; in awakening to soberness they will escape the intoxicating snare. "The devil's method of taking men captive is to benumb the conscience, confuse the senses, and paralyse the will" (Horton). As men who are drunken, they are unable to free themselves from the snare of the Devil.

The concluding phrase, "having been taken captive by him unto his will," describes their resultant condition as captured by the Devil. The words have been variously interpreted. Literally translated they read, "having been taken captive by him unto the will of that one." It is the use of the two different pronouns that has raised the questions. Whom does Paul mean by "him" and by "that one"? Some would refer "him" to the servant of the Lord (v.24) and "that one" to God (v.25). But that makes the antecedent for "him" too remote. Others take "him" to mean the Devil and "that one" God. Both of these views arise from the feeling that the two pronouns cannot refer to the same subject. The common view has been to refer both pronouns to the same subject, namely, the Devil. The antecedent of "him" is naturally the nearest noun, the Devil, while the demonstrative pronoun "that one" most naturally refers again to the nearest pronoun "him," having the force of "that person, that notorious character" (Boise). The difference in the two pronouns is no real objection against this view when it is recognized that the change in the pronoun is for the sake of emphasis. That notorious enemy, the Devil, has captured them with the intention of keeping them permanently captive (perfect tense) to do "his will," instead of God's will. If men will not be the servants of God they inevitably become the captives of the Devil. Man's freedom is his freedom to choose his master.

2. *The Minister and the Coming Apostasy,* 3:1-17

But know this, that in the last days grievous times shall come. For men shall be lovers of self, lovers of money, boastful, haughty, railers, disobedient to parents, unthankful, unholy, without natural affection, implacable, slanderers, without self-control, fierce, no lovers of good, traitors, headstrong, puffed up, lovers of pleasure rather than lovers of God; holding a form of godliness, but having denied the power thereof: from these also turn away. For of these are they that creep into houses, and take captive silly women laden with sins, led away by divers lusts, ever learning, and never able to come to the knowledge of the truth. And even as Jannes and Jambres withstood Moses, so do these also withstand the truth; men corrupted in mind, reprobate concerning the faith. But they shall proceed no further: for their

80

folly shall be evident unto all men, as theirs also came to be.

But thou didst follow my teaching, conduct, purpose, faith, longsuffering, love, patience, persecutions, sufferings; what things befell me at Antioch, at Iconium, at Lystra; what persecutions I endured: and out of them all the Lord delivered me. Yea, and all that would live godly in Christ Jesus shall suffer persecutions. But evil men and impostors shall wax worse and worse, deceiving and being deceived. But abide thou in the things which thou hast learned and hast been assured of, knowing of whom thou hast learned them; and that from a babe thou hast known the sacred writings which are able to make thee wise unto salvation through faith which is in Christ Jesus. Every scripture inspired of God is also profitable for teaching, for reproof, for correction, for instruction which is in righteousness: that the man of God may be complete, furnished completely unto every good work.

Having set before Timothy the minister's reaction to doctrinal error about him, Paul next turns his thoughts to the still darker future. To fortify Timothy, Paul records the prophecy of the coming apostasy (vv. 1-9) and then holds up before him the power to meet the apostasy (vv. 10-17).

a. The prophecy concerning the apostasy, vv. 1-9. Paul is not merely offering shrewd deductions of his own from contemporary trends but is speaking by revelation. Paul announces the fact of the coming apostasy (v. 1), gives a vivid delineation of the coming moral depravity (vv. 2-5a), issues a summary command to turn away from such people (v. 5b), and graphically pictures the work of such apostates (vv. 6-9).

1) The announcement of the coming grievous times, v. 1. "But know this, that in the last days grievous times shall come." Notwithstanding the hope just expressed for

the recovery of those who have been caught in the Devil's snare (2:24-26), Timothy must realize that opposition to the truth will grow even more intense and that evil men will arise in the professed circle of believers who will not be redeemed. With the present imperative, "this know," Timothy is told to keep this realization before him. The one point stressed is the fact that "grievous times," hard and difficult seasons, lie ahead when believers will be confronted with perplexing problems and difficult duties because of the abounding iniquity operating under the pretense of being Christian. The time indicated is "in the last days." The original does not have the article, thus designating a characteristic state, rather than a positive time. It is not to be limited to the few years just before the Second Advent. The use of the article would have made the period too restricted; its absence enlarges the sphere to cover the closing seasons of the Christian era, however long God may be pleased to protract them. The seeds of the evil being predicted were already sprouting when Paul wrote, but the evil will find its awful culmination in the closing seasons of this age. There have been repeated incipient fulfillments when believers felt that the prophecy was a description of their own times. Every informed believer is painfully aware of the fearful apostasy that is sweeping over Christendom in our own times. This prophecy was recorded as God's advance warning to His servants to fortify them as they confront apostasy in their own day.

2) The description of the coming apostates, vv. 2-5a. Paul gives a graphic description of the moral depravity that is coming (vv. 2-4) and concludes the picture with a reference to the religious profession of these apostates (v. 5a).

a) The description of their character, vv. 2-4. The

coming seasons will be so difficult because of the evil people living in them. "For men shall be—." The Greek has the definite article "the men," that is, the people generally (not just the men as contrasted to the women). The implication is that the majority of the people at that time will be such as he indicates, although not all of these traits need be thought of as being combined in any single individual. Some of the traits will be outstanding in some people, while others will be prominent in other people. In typical Pauline fashion, a fearful catalogue of their iniquitous traits is given. Counting as one the concluding double feature in verse 4, we have eighteen characteristics listed. Efforts to group these traits to show logical sequence have not been too successful. They obviously form one sordid picture, but some of the elements are more closely connected than others. As Lenski remarks: "Paul is not dividing these people into so many groups, for these groups would always run together like liquids."

The first two traits naturally go together. (1) "Lovers of self" aptly heads the list since it is the essence of all sin and the root from which all the other characteristics spring. The word is literally "self-lovers" and points to the fact that the center of gravity of the natural man is self rather than God. (2) "Lovers of money" naturally follows as indicating the means for the gratification of self. In Luke 16:14, the only other use of the word in the New Testament, it is used to describe the arrogant Pharisees.

The next three terms are closely related, "boastful, haughty, railers." Being (3) "boastful" they indulge in bragging about themselves and arrogate to themselves honors which do not rightly belong to them. In their supposed superiority they are (4) "haughty," overbearing in their relations to others, and in their disdain of others they become (5) "railers," literally "blasphemers." Their speech is abusive and injurious of others. They resort to scornful language, insulting both men and God.

The next characteristic (6) "disobedient to parents," constitutes the fountal sin for their disregard of all authority. If children do not learn to obey their parents, whom God has set over them, it is not likely that they will be obedient to other authority, whether human or divine. This is a frightful characteristic of our own time. Their unfilial attitude and actions naturally lead them to be (7) "unthankful." They are unappreciative of all the benefits which they have received from their parents. This unthankfulness naturally extends itself in their response to other human benefactors, and to God Himself. In their unthankfulness, they become (8) "unholy," impious, respecting and revering nothing as sacred. The word describes their disregard of their duty toward God. These characteristics stamp them as being (9) "without natural affection," as "destitute of love toward those for whom nature herself claims it" (Ellicott). By their indifference to and utter disregard for the welfare of those with whom they are connected by natural ties they sink lower than the beasts. Their callousness makes them (10) "implacable," irreconcilable, refusing to enter into a truce to terminate a state of hostilities. "Their feuds never end. In their camp no libation is ever poured out to signify that those who had been at variance with each other have consented to a truce" (Hendriksen). The thought is not that they break their truce, but that they resist all efforts to reconciliation. Their viciousness manifests itself in being (11) "slanderers," that is, false accusers. The term, which is literally "devils," points out the fact that they imitate the Devil himself in constantly inventing and throwing across evil reports and accusations at others.

84

The next three characteristics constitute a descending triad. They are (12) "without self-control," having never learned to exercise a restraint upon their lusts and passions. They are devoid of that inner power of self-government which is the characteristic of the disciplined man. They are (13) "fierce," savage and untamed like wild animals in their attitudes and actions. Being wild and untamed, they sink to the place where they are (14) "no lovers of good." It may mean that they have no love for good men, but probably, more generally, it means that they have no love for virtue, no love for that which is good or beneficial to others.

The next three traits again are closely related vices. They are (15) "traitors," betraying confidence and trust put in them. Perhaps the reference is to their betrayal of other Christians to the persecutors. The man who can betray his friends will not hesitate to throw off other restraints, and so they become (16) "headstrong," literally, "such as fall forward." They are rash and reckless and plunge ahead without forethought in their impetuous deeds. They end up by having their moral nature utterly blinded, being (17) "puffed up." The perfect participle pictures them as being in a state of being blinded by their pride and conceit. No one can tell them anything, for they know it all.

The last of the characterizations of their moral depravity is composed of two "lover" traits which are in antagonism to each other. They are (18) "lovers of pleasure rather than lovers of God." They love their own pleasures and are wholly controlled by them. They are willing to make any sacrifice for temporal pleasures but are unwilling to give up anything because of their love for God. They put devotion to self-satisfaction above devotion to God. Love for God is not a controlling motive in their lives. The series began with their love of self and ends with their lack of love for God. Their love of self with all its attendant evils shuts out any genuine love for God.

b) The description of their religion, v. 5a. "Holding a form of godliness, but having denied the power thereof." They are not self-acknowledged pagans but rather professed adherents of Christianity. They maintain a form of piety which looks as though it corresponds to the essence but there is a lack of the true substance. Their profession is useless and powerless because by their depraved and vicious actions they have contradicted their outward show and profession of godliness. The perfect tense "having denied" indicates that they have done so and still continue to do so by the way they live.

This list has much in common with that found in Romans 1, but there is a tragic difference. There Paul draws the dark picture of an unenlightened heathenism, but here the picture is that of "a society enjoying the light of the Christian revelation and whose sinning is rendered all the more heinous through its knowledge of the truth" (Pope). It is the fearful portrayal of an apostate Christendom, a new paganism masquerading under the name of Christianity.

3) The command to separate from apostates, v. 5b. "From these also turn away." The force of the original means that Timothy must habitually "turn himself away from" people like this. The word rendered "also" stands at the beginning of the sentence: "And from these turn away." It joins this duty with that mentioned in verse 1. To keep on realizing and turning away from such people is his only course of safety amid apostasy. This stands in striking contrast to the instructions given Timothy in 2:25, when dealing with those who had been ensnared in

error. But these men have "reached a stage of deprava-
tion where instruction is useless or impracticable. They
must be avoided" (Harvey).

This exhortation clearly implies that Paul did not consider the state of moral depravity just pictured as wholly
a matter of the future. He was keenly aware that the
evils about which he was forewarning were already at
work. As Ellicott remarks:

> The seeds of all these evils were germinating even at
> the present time; and Timothy, by being supplied with
> criteria derived from the *developed future,* was to be
> warned in regard of the *developing present.*

4) The work of the apostates, vv. 6-9. In verses 2-5
we have the general picture; here attention is drawn to a
particular kind of such evil men. Paul describes their
activities (v. 6a), their victims (vv. 6b, 7), and their
character (v. 8), and assures Timothy of the limitation
upon their success (v. 9).

a) The description of their work, v. 6a. "For of these
are they that creep into houses, and take captive silly
women." These men come out of the circles of those just
described. Their activities are described by two present
participles of characteristic action, "creeping into houses
and taking captive." Like serpents or wolves they "creep
into houses" or households seeking their prey. Their actions are characterized by a certain stealth and secretive-
ness. They specialize in the art of captivating women. In
seeking to gain some household as their followers they
make special efforts to win converts among the women.
By means of their winsome manners and their plausible
propaganda they bring these women wholly under their
evil influences.

b) The victims of their work, vv. 6b, 7. Their victims
are designated as "silly women." The original word is a

neuter diminutive expressive of contempt, "womanlings."
It speaks of the contemptible state into which they have
fallen. Four descriptive participles picture these women:

(1) "laden with sins." The perfect tense pictures them as
being in a state of "being heaped up with sins." Their
conscience is loaded with many sins of great variety.
Uneasy about the consequences of their sins they are re-
ceptive to these false propagandists who come to them
with their attractive panaceas. (2) "Led away by divers
lusts." They continue to be governed in their conduct by
a motley array of desires and cravings. What these desires
were is not stated, but they are pictured as being "divers," that is, "many colored," of great variety. These
lusts must not be restricted to sexual desire. Included are
the desire to be considered "well-informed," to receive
the flattering personal attention of these professed teachers of new and advanced truth, the craving for new experiences that would flatter their ego. Hence they are
further described as (3) "ever learning," at every opportunity eager to receive instruction from anyone who will
undertake to teach them. In their restless quest for the
new and novel they turn to every new doctrine that comes
to their attention. The apostle adds (4) "and never able
to come to the knowledge of the truth." The words
"never able" suggests an abiding inability on their part to
come to an effective realization of the truth of the Gospel.
"In their better moments they might endeavor to attain to
some knowledge of the truth, but they never succeed"
(Ellicott). By following teachers who lead them away
from the Gospel they never come to know it. "Running
after error and at the same time living in sin is not a
good way to find the truth" (Greene).

c) The character of these apostates, v. 8. From a description of their victims Paul turns to a presentation of

their own character. By comparing them to the Egyptian court magicians he describes their conduct as giving a revelation of their attitude. "And even as Jannes and Jambres withstood Moses, so do these also withstand the truth." The names of these two men, the chief Egyptian magicians who opposed Moses, are not given in Exodus, but these names were familiar to Jewish tradition. Paul's use of these names has caused much discussion as to their origin and authenticity. But as Ellicott remarks:

> Objections urged against the introduction of these names, when gravely considered, will be found of no weight whatever; why was the inspired apostle not to remind Timothy of the ancient traditions of his country, and to cite two names which there is every reason to suppose were too closely connected with the early history of the nation to be easily forgotten?

The expressed point in the comparison is their opposition to the truth. As Jannes and Jambres in Egypt sought to oppose the truth of God by means of their counterfeit miracles, so these self-seeking, fraudulent men now oppose the truth of the Gospel. The fact that Paul compares these men to the Egyptian magicians, although not directly stated, seems to make it a consistent assumption that these men likewise availed themselves of occult powers and practices. They may have been people who before their professed conversion to Christianity had practiced magical arts. Thus Harvey concludes: "They directly opposed the true gospel by setting up their magical arts in rivalry with the gifts of the Spirit, as the old Egyptian sorcerers had done in the contest with Moses."

Their opposition, as the following words show, revealed their corrupt mind and their failure in the matter of the faith. "Men corrupted in mind" pictures their utter moral depravity. The perfect tense points to the permanent state of their corruption, while the passive voice implies an agent, the Devil, who led them to their corruption. Their "mind," the God-given "faculty of perceiving and understanding," the channel through which truth reaches the heart, has become corrupted so that the truth cannot get through to them. They have become "reprobate concerning the faith." "Reprobate" means that they have been tested in regard to "the faith," the Christian teaching, and like counterfeit coin have been found wanting, hence must be discarded as worthless. The truth which they claim to bring in their teaching, upon examination, is found to be counterfeit gold.

d) The limitation upon their work, v. 9. The comparison of these men with Jannes and Jambres leads Paul to make another observation. "But they shall proceed no further: for their folly shall be evident unto all men, as theirs also came to be." The concluding words, "as theirs also," remind Timothy that as the counterfeit claims of Jannes and Jambres were exposed before the entire court, so the success of these men will likewise be limited. Paul asserts, "they shall proceed no further." Although they will grow worse in their own moral depravity, as 3:13 indicates, they will not succeed in making further spectacular gains in their pernicious influence over others. The reason is, "for their folly shall be evident unto all men." Their "folly," their senselessness and lack of understanding, derived from their wickedness, will become clear to all. Christians are the first to recognize this, but others also over whom they have exercised their influence will come to see it. Absurdity and fraud eventually overstep their bounds and thus expose their folly.

b. The power to meet the coming apostasy, vv. 10-17. With this ghastly picture of the coming grievous times before him, Paul turns directly to Timothy to remind him of the resources available enabling him to stand true. He will find strength and encouragement in the remembrance of his past association with Paul (vv. 10-13), but the final source of power to withstand in the coming evil days lies in the functional nature of Holy Scripture (vv. 14-17).

1) The remembrance of Paul's sufferings, vv. 10-13. Paul turns directly to Timothy with a word of emphatic personal address; "but thou," setting Timothy in sharp contrast to the men just described. In his associations with Paul, Timothy has been following a manner of life the very opposite of them. Paul gives a terse description of his life and its sufferings (vv. 10, 11) and gives an explanation for such sufferings (vv. 12, 13).

a) The reminder of his life and sufferings, vv. 10, 11. In view of his impending death the aged apostle reminds Timothy of their past relationship. "Thou didst follow" points out the essential nature of that relationship. Paul was the leader, guiding and directing, Timothy was the loving, trusting, sympathetic follower, assistant and friend. But that precious relationship will soon be terminated and Timothy will need to stand alone. The compound form of the verb means literally "to follow alongside, to follow closely," and thus intimates his diligent tracing of that life step by step. The verb does not imply that Timothy has always been at the side of Paul but that he has observed that life with close interest. Yet none of Paul's numerous companions seem to have been more continuously associated with Paul personally than Timothy. The tense of the verb states the historical fact of that close relationship between them.

Paul employs nine terms to give a graphic sketch of his past career, a career wholly devoted to the service of Christ. "My teaching, conduct, purpose, faith, longsuffering, love, patience, persecutions, sufferings." The original has the definite article with each word, thus setting each item off as distinct, but all preceded by the pronoun "my." To get the force of it we should repeat "my" with each word. There is neither egotism nor boasting in this compressed biography. Paul's purpose in thus setting forth his life and sufferings is to stir Timothy with renewed determination to face the difficulties of life in the same resolute and devoted spirit.

Attempts to discover groups in these nine particulars have not been very successful, but an order of sequence is evident. He logically begins with (1) "my teaching," that is, the Gospel message which he is proclaiming. That is the basis and ground of all else. His teaching was done by word of mouth, hence he next mentions (2) his "conduct." The original word, used only here in the New Testament, points to the guiding principles of Paul's life but as these found expression is his actual conduct. As the apostle of Christ, Paul was keenly aware that he taught not only by his word but also by his conduct (cf. Acts 20:18-35; I Thess. 2:1-12; I Cor. 11:1). There is no better comment on the inspired Word than the consistent conduct of the one who proclaims it. The harmony between Paul's teaching and conduct left no doubt as to the sincerity of (3) his "purpose," that steadfast purpose in Paul to devote his life unceasingly to the furtherance of the Gospel. With such consistent clarity did this purpose shine in Paul's life that only the malignant and the willfully blind could misinterpret it. The motivating power of his life was (4) his "faith." The word may here mean "faithfulness," his fidelity, but it is more probable that the word has its usual meaning of "faith," his own faith or trust in God and His Word. It was this faith that kept alive the fire in the heart of the apostle amid all of his afflictions. Paul's work did not always receive a kindly reception, therefore in his dealings with opposers and erring brethren Timothy had seen Paul's (5) "longsuffering." Such patient forbearance with sinners and even persecutors is indeed the fruit of the Spirit of God. His dealings with all classes of people had revealed (6) his "love" to men. It was a love for friend and foe alike, born of the Holy Spirit shed abroad in his heart. Put to the test in various forms and in varying degrees, there had been (7) "patience," namely, steadfast perseverance amid trying circumstances. Amid suffering and adverse experiences he had had the grace bravely to endure, to bear up under the load. And that attitude of brave patience had been brought into open manifestation through the (8) numerous "persecutions" he had experienced. As a natural effect, these persecutions caused (9) his "sufferings."

His sufferings Paul next describes by two qualitative phrases. The first is indefinite as to the nature of the sufferings: "what [kind of] things befell me at Antioch, at Iconium, at Lystra." For a description of the sufferings alluded to read Acts 13 and 14. Now at the end of his life, as the apostle reviews his experiences, it is only natural that he should again think of the sharp sufferings endured on the first missionary journey. It was in connection with the experiences of this journey that Timothy first became acquainted with Paul. It may be that he mentions them here because, due to their severity, they were typical of his subsequent experiences. It is very likely that Timothy had himself seen the stoning which Paul underwent at Lystra, Timothy's home town. The second qualifying clause points to the intensity of his sufferings, "what [kind of] persecutions I endured." They had been sharp and bitter indeed. (For a longer list of

Paul's experiences see II Corinthians 11:24-27.) But Paul at once adds a note of encouragement for Timothy, "and out of them all the Lord delivered me." The "and" (not "but" as in the King James Version) marks this deliverance not as a strange but the normal and expected thing. "The preservation of Christ's faithful servant had been even more conspicuous than his sufferings" (Harvey). The Lord does not promise to keep His servants "from" suffering but He delivers them "out" of it. "The Lord *ever* rescues His people, frequently *from* death, sometimes *by means of* death. Either way, nothing ever separates them from His love (Rom. 8:38, 39)" (Hendriksen).

b) The explanation for such suffering, vv. 12, 13. The first explanation for his sufferings lies in the fact that it is the lot of all the godly. His experiences are nothing extraordinary and exceptional. "Yea, and all that would live godly in Christ Jesus shall suffer persecution." The words "that would" point to those whose will is enlisted in the matter, those who have made it an abiding determination to live a godly life. But such a life is not native to the human heart; it can only be lived "in Christ Jesus," in vital spiritual union with Him. It is the only source and sphere of a truly godly life. "The 'godly' indicates the Christian life on its ethical side in the life of conduct; the words 'in Christ' give the other aspect of the Christian life—its inner, mystic fellowship with Christ" (Pope).

Because of the abiding antagonism of the world to vital godliness, persecution is the natural lot of the godly. The persecution of the godly by the world may vary in degree and take different forms in different countries and in different ages, but the basic hostility of the world to the godly man remains unchanged. As Horton well remarks:

94

The life of Christ, in which the believer shares, is a life which, if not against, is always athwart, the world. Its motives and springs, its standards and precepts, its modes and developments, its goal and its ends, are as different from the world's as light is from darkness. And as day and night are the perpetual battle between the light and the darkness, so the Christian life is an unceasing struggle against principalities and powers, and the rulers of the darkness of this world.

A further explanation of the suffering of the godly is to be found in the fact of the growing degeneracy of the wicked. This antagonism to the godly will not diminish because "evil men and impostors shall wax worse and worse." Verse 13 does not offer a contrast to verse 12 as the opening "but" of our versions implies. This verse presents the reason why the persecutions of Christians will not cease. These "evil men and impostors" are the ones described in verses 2-9 above, or more precisely we may say that the "evil men" are depicted in verses 2-5 and the "impostors" in verses 6-9. The latter, in keeping with the reference to Jannes and Jambres, are designated "impostors," literally, "sorcerers, or magicians." The use of the word would seem to imply again (cf. on v. 8 above) that they were practitioners of occult arts, spiritualists of a sort. The evangelical believer needs to be alert to the machinations of modern spiritualism, especially to that misnomer called "Christian Spiritualism." Of such men Paul asserts that they "shall wax worse and worse." The verb rendered "wax" is translated "proceed" in verse 9 above, as well as in 2:16, and means "to cut forward, to advance." Claiming to be "progressive," they will make progress, but only in inward moral and spiritual degeneracy. "Though the spread of the evil may be repressed by the early exposure of these men, yet the men themselves will go from bad to worse, according to the natural tendency of error and sin" (Harvey). Paul adds the terse description, "deceiving and being deceived," the present tenses denoting the continuing action. The two actions go together. They begin by deceiving others, but in doing so they lose their sense of the distinction between truth and falsehood, and eventually they end up by being deceived by the deceptions of others. Thus sin brings its own punishment.

2) The stand in the power of the Scriptures, vv. 14-17. Again, as in verse 10, Paul turns directly to Timothy with a word of personal appeal. "But . . . thou" sets Timothy in definite contrast to these deceivers. He will find the power to stand in his adherence to his experiential relation to the Scriptures. The remembrance of Paul's heroic sufferings, as well as the realization that suffering is the lot of all believers, will undergird Timothy's endurance. But the ultimate source of his power to stand firm he must find in the Scriptures. Paul reminds him of his subjective experience with the Sacred Writings (vv. 14, 15) and asserts the objective fact of the nature and function of the Scriptures (vv. 16, 17).

a) The experience of Timothy with the Scriptures, vv. 14, 15. The deepening degradation of these self-willed deceivers makes it imperative that Timothy firmly adhere to the divine truths which he has accepted. "Abide thou in the things which thou hast learned and hast been assured of." He must ever "abide," or remain in these things, and not advance away from them, like these false teachers. This does not prohibit his moral, spiritual, or intellectual progress, but all true progress must be within, not away from, the divine fundamentals of the Christian revelation. These sacred truths Timothy has learned and has been assured of. The aorist tenses summarily state the past historic facts. The latter verb "hast been assured of," "hast been firmly persuaded of," points to that inner conviction concerning the truth and reality of these things which has come to him. Such an assurance produces personal stability. Doubts and uncertainties concerning the Word of God never foster moral steadfastness.

Paul reminds Timothy of the teachers from whom he has learned these Christian verities. "Knowing of whom thou hast learned them." In some manuscripts the word for "whom" is in the singular; this would mean that he has learned these Gospel truths from Paul himself. But the best manuscripts have the plural. Then the meaning is that not only Paul but his esteemed mother and grandmother have shared in imparting these truths to Timothy. He has not received the knowledge of the truth from an unknown or suspicious source. The content of the teaching received is very important, but so also is the character of the teacher. His personal knowledge of his teachers assures him of the reliability of the things he has learned.

But Timothy's knowledge of things divine was not derived merely from human teachers, however esteemed and trustworthy. He has had the great advantage of a thorough training in the Holy Scriptures from early childhood. "And that from a babe thou hast known the sacred writings." "From a babe" points to the very early age at which his instruction in the Scriptures began. Jewish children were taught to memorize passages from the Old Testament as soon as they could speak. The ultimate source and authority for his religious faith was the Word of God. The verb "hast known" has the force of the present tense and denotes continuous action. His knowledge, begun in earliest childhood, continues through to the present time. He cannot recall a period when he did not know the sacred writings, and he has continued to know them better and better. By "the sacred writings" Paul means the recognized Hebrew Scriptures, not merely religious literature in general. The adjective "sacred" points to the esteem and veneration in which the Hebrew Scriptures were held by the Jews and the Christian churches. From such a source Timothy had gotten his knowledge of things divine.

The value of knowing these "sacred writings" lies in the fact that they are able to do what no secular writings can do, namely, "which are able to make thee wise unto salvation." The present tense of the participle rendered "which are able" points to the continuous and abiding power resident in these writings. Not only were they able to do so in the case of Timothy, but they continue to make "wise," to enlighten and instruct those instructed therein. The Holy Scriptures have an abiding power on the human heart. But the words "unto salvation" at once indicate the kind of wisdom which the Scriptures impart. As Bernard remarks:

> The significance of the O. T. is not that it contains an account of the creation of man or the history of the fortunes of Israel; its aim is not *knowledge,* whether scientific or historical, but *wisdom,* and that *unto salvation. Salvation,* the salvation of man, is the final purpose of the whole Bible.

But an intellectual apprehension of the truths of Scripture does not assure salvation. There is no magical power in the Scriptures which guarantee personal salvation to those knowing their contents. Rather, "the truths of Scripture present to the mind the true objects of faith, and are the medium through which the Holy Spirit exerts his renewing, saving power" (Harvey). And this requires that there be a personal appropriation through faith on our part, as Paul immediately indicates by adding, "through faith which is in Christ Jesus." Saving faith centers in and rests upon Christ as revealed in the Scriptures. Faith is the means through which the salvation expounded in the Word is grasped. Faith in Christ is the link which unites the Old and the New Testaments. The Old Testament Scriptures must be studied in the light of the revelation which was made in Christ Jesus. As Van Oosterzee observes:

> Not every one can be made wise unto salvation by the writings of the Old Covenant, but only every one who believes in Christ. Faith in Christ is, as it were, a torch, by the light of which we can first read aright and understand the dim colonnades and mysterious inscriptions in the ancient venerable temple of the Old Covenant.

b) The nature and function of the Scriptures, vv. 16, 17. The appeal to Timothy in verse 14 to "abide," which Paul strengthened by a reference to Timothy's subjective experience with the sacred writings, is now further strengthened by an objective statement concerning the nature and function of Scripture. "Every scripture inspired of God is also profitable." The absence of any word for "is" in the original makes possible two different translations, and interpreters have been divided on the matter ever since the day of Origen. It is grammatically and exegetically possible to translate "every scripture is inspired of God and profitable," or "every Scripture, inspired of God, is also profitable." In the former translation the inspiration of Scripture is asserted, while in the latter it is assumed. But the latter rendering must not be construed to imply that there are some parts or some books of Scripture which are not inspired.

Both of these renderings have their advocates. In favor of the latter rendering it is held that the inspiration of Scripture was not in question and to assert it would be uncalled for. But there is nothing against the view that Paul would seek to confirm the soul of Timothy in view of the coming perilous times with an assertion of the inspiration as well as of the profitableness of Scripture. The translation of the conjunction as "also," although this is a common meaning, seems rather harsh here; it seems more natural to regard it as the connective between two predicates, "is inspired *and* profitable." We accept the former rendering, "every scripture is inspired of God and profitable," as the more probable reading.

The subject is without the article and would commonly mean "every scripture," every single part of it; but if "every scripture" is inspired then Scripture in its entirety is also inspired, hence "all scripture" is equally possible as a rendering. "Every scripture" views the individual parts, while "all scripture" views it in its totality. The word "scripture," either in the plural or in the singular (as here), is used more than fifty times in the New Testament to denote the Old Testament Scriptures as received by the Jews in the days of Christ and the apostles. In verse 15 the reference was to the "sacred writings," denoting the Hebrew Scriptures; here the word "scripture" without the article is more general and leaves room for other writings that have a right to be called divinely inspired Scriptures

The word rendered "inspired of God," used only heie in the New Testament, is literally "God-breathed." It points to the fact that Scripture owes its origin and character to the living Spirit of God. Lilley comments:

Since the breath of God is everywhere identified with His presence, the epithet as applied to the Scriptures can only mean that, written by holy men of old borne on by the Holy Spirit, every scripture has the presence and operation of God indissolubly associated with it; and that this gracious influence of the Spirit as the direct Agent at work will be felt by every one that reads them with a humble and teachable heart.

This inspiration is here not asserted of the authors of Scripture but of the writings themselves. But inspiration was not mechanical. The Holy Spirit did not destroy the personality and individual characteristics of the individual writers but rather so worked through the entire being of the writer that the very words used, although truly the words of the human author, were yet the very words the Spirit intended to be employed to express the divine truths being recorded. The present imperfect condition of the Biblical text, which has suffered in its transmission through fallible scribes, is no ground for concluding against the original text being inspired. It is rather a reason why all critical diligence should be applied to seek to restore the original inspired text as nearly as possible.

The verbal translated "inspired of God" (*theopneustos*) is not active in meaning, "God-breathing, breathing the divine spirit." The teaching is not that the Scriptures are inspired whenever they breathe the presence of God to us. The verbal is passive in meaning and the agent breathing into the Scriptures was God Himself, making them "God-breathed," that is, inspired. Such is their abiding character.

Since every Scripture is God-breathed it follows that it is "also profitable," proving serviceable to the moral and spiritual needs of man. Their profitableness attests their inspiration. This profitableness is expanded in four points: (1) "for teaching," for instruction in doctrinal truth. The Bible is our supreme source for our knowledge concerning God's revelation in Christ. (2) "For reproof," detecting and exposing all that is false. It convicts all that is unholy and all ungodly men, exposing and refuting every religious error and falsehood. (3) "For correction," or restoration. It restores the fallen sinner to an upright position and sets the erring one again on the right path. (4) "For instruction which is in righteousness," providing the discipline that is needed in the sphere of righteousness. The word rendered "instruction" is literally "child-training." Every believer, like a child, needs to be educated, trained and disciplined in righteousness, so that he may prosper in this sphere where righteousness is the norm of life.

The profitablenss of inspired Scripture is set forth in its contemplated result, "that the man of God may be complete, furnished completely unto every good work." The expression "the man of God" is here not an official designation but denotes every believer viewed as belonging to God, for Paul has not been speaking about ministers in relation to the Word but the work of the Scriptures generally. The goal is that the believer, trained by the inspired Word, may be "complete," "complete in all parts and proportions" (Ellicott). This thought of his harmonious equipment is repeated in the added participle "furnished completely," the perfect tense denoting this as his abiding condition. There is to be no lack of proportion or balance in any area of his being. As such he will be permanently equipped "unto every good work," every work that is intrinsically good. Wherever it is allowed to have its intended result, "instruction by the Scripture will secure for every believer continuous, growing, inward capacity and readiness for the accomplishment of everying pleasing to the Lord" (Van Oosterzee).

3. *The Final Charge to Timothy, 4:1-8*

I charge thee in the sight of God, and of Christ Jesus, who shall judge the living and the dead, and by his appearing and his kingdom: preach the word; be urgent in season, out of season; reprove, rebuke, exhort, with all longsuffering and teaching. For the time will come when they will not endure the sound doctrine; but, having itching ears, will heap to themselves teachers after their own lusts; and will turn away their ears from the truth, and turn aside unto fables. But be thou sober in all things, suffer hardship, do the work of an evangelist, fulfill thy ministry. For I am already being offered, and the time of my departure is come. I have fought the good fight, I have finished the course, I have kept the faith: henceforth there is laid up for me the crown of righteousness, which the Lord, the righteous judge, shall give to me at that day; and not to me only, but also to all them that have loved his appearing.

In this solemn, stirring paragraph, containing a double statement of the charge to Timothy, we reach the grand climax of the epistle. With studied solemnity Paul recapitulates the previous admonitions, conscious that not improbably it may be the very last charge he will ever give to this beloved son. With deep feeling he lays upon him the charge to preach the Word (vv. 1-4), and again, soberly to fulfill his ministry (vv. 5-8).

a. The charge to preach the Word, vv. 1-4. Paul emphatically indicates the solemnity of the charge (v. 1), makes the statement of the charge (v. 2), and indicates the reason for the charge (vv. 3, 4).

1) The solemnity in making the charge, v. 1. "I charge thee in the sight of God, and of Christ Jesus." "I charge," or "I solemnly order, adjure," indicates that he is laying a mandate upon Timothy which must be obeyed. And he does so "in the sight of God, and of Christ Jesus," thus summoning him, as it were, into the presence of God the Father and of the glorified Son of God to receive the charge. Christ Jesus is set before him as the coming Judge, "who shall judge the living and the dead."

The words "shall judge" more literally are "is about to be judging"; they point to the fact that Paul was living in the hope of the imminent return of Christ. At His return He will be judging "the living," the inhabitants of the earth at that time, as well as "the dead," those who have died and passed from this earth. The present tense of the verb "judge," denoting repeated action, takes in the various judgments to come in connection with the living and the dead. Paul continues the charge by saying "and by his appearing and his kingdom." Here are additional facts the contemplation of which must stimulate Timothy to faithfulness in his work. Here the thought advances to the future visible return of Christ and the kingdom which He will set up at His coming. (The reading in the King James, "at his appearing," which connects the phrase with "shall judge," follows a different reading. The oldest manuscripts read "and" rather than the preposition producing the rendering "at.")

2) The statement of the charge, v. 2. By means of five brisk imperatives, all in the aorist tense and without connecting particles, the duty of Timothy is set forth with the force of peremptory military commands. The tense implies prompt action. "Preach the word," that is, the Word of God, the Gospel. This stands first as the very heart and center of his work. This is man's supreme need and it is his highest and primary task. But the verb "preach" does not necessarily imply an ordained minister preaching from a stately church pulpit. The original verb has in it the picture of a herald making a public proclamation as ordered by another. The word would bring to Timothy's mind the picture of "the Imperial Herald, spokesman of the Emperor, proclaiming in a formal, grave, and authoritative manner which must be listened to, the message which the Emperor gave him to an-

nounce" (Wuest). The King of Heaven has committed His message to His messengers and it is their duty faithfully and with proper dignity to proclaim that message to men without alteration or falsification.

The next command brings out the needed insistency in the work, "be urgent in season, out of season." The verb rendered "be urgent" means "to stand by, to be at hand," to be "on the spot" as we say. Ellicott remarks that it "appears to mark an attitude of prompt attention that may at any moment pass into action." The minister must hold himself in constant readiness to proclaim the message entrusted to him. And he must be at work "in season, out of season," whether the circumstances appear "opportune" or "inopportune." "He who desires to wait until the occasion seems completely favourable for his work, will never find it" (Huther).

Three commands follow in rapid succession setting forth the specifications of his work, "reprove, rebuke, exhort." "Reprove," or convict those who are erring from the truth or failing in holiness. "Rebuke" is a stronger word, "chide, censure, blame." He must reprimand the sinner and not tone down his sin. His work also requires that he "exhort," that is, admonish or encourage. He must give tender, sympathetic admonition and encouragement to the fainthearted and the discouraged. The added phrase "with all longsuffering and teaching" relates to all three of these duties. His work must be characterized by an attitude of the utmost longsuffering and self-restraint, resisting every temptation to impatient anger at the obstinacy and perverseness of those being dealt with. To be profitable the rebuke and exhortation must be accompanied with "teaching," sound and reasonable instruction in the truth. "Evil and falsehood are less effectually dispelled by controversy than by the presentation of the good and the true" (Bernard).

3) The reason for the charge, vv. 3, 4. Paul draws an argument for present diligence in preaching from the prospect of a darker future. "For the time will come when they will not endure the sound doctrine." Paul's prophetic statement is clearly a description of a condition that will characterize, not the world in general, but professing Christendom. The time will come when professed Christians "will not endure," will not tolerate, put up with "the sound doctrine," that is, healthful, useful, practical teaching from the Word of God giving health and soundness to the spiritual man. They will find the truth of God so intolerable because its demands are contrary to their own desires. The Word is the touchstone that reveals their true character.

Their negative reaction inevitably leads to a positive course of action. "But, having itching ears, will heap to themselves teachers after their own lusts." The people are described as having "itching ears." (The American Standard Version transposes this expression to show that it refers to the people, not to the teachers.) The reason for their intolerance toward God's Word lies not in the heralds of that divine message but in the attitude of the people. The expression "having itching ears" points to that incessant, unsatisfied craving for the new and the novel which dominates them. They yearn for pleasurable excitement by having their ears tickled by the latest fancies and speculations of "scholarship." "Hardly has the latest novelty been toyed with, than it is cast aside as stale and frayed, and a newer is sought" (Ernest Gordon, quoted in Wuest). It is an apt picture of the spirit of Modernism with its rejection of the finality of the Christian revelation, its insistence upon the relativity of truth, and its unending parade of "advanced" insights and professed discoveries of new truth. To satisfy their cravings, Paul continues, they "will heap to themselves teachers after their own lusts." And they will find plenty of teachers who are willing to satisfy their demands that their ears be tickled with their new fancies, but their standard for their multiplication of their teachers is "their own lusts." Teachers are chosen not because of their faithful adherence to the Gospel but because of their ability to tickle their itching ears.

The result of this craving is that they "will turn away their ears from the truth, and turn aside unto fables." Since faithful preachers of the Gospel will not gratify their itch for the novel and fanciful, they will deliberately turn from such teachers and "turn aside unto fables." The second verb rendered "turn" is a stronger word than the first and means "to turn or twist out." In medical terminology it was used of wrenching a limb out of joint. They will twist themselves out of their normal position in order to have their itching ears gratified with "fables," fictitious inventions as opposed to fact. Such idle tales are more pleasing to them than the Gospel with its rebuke for sin and its demands for holiness of life.

These "fables" are not here qualified as being "Jewish" as in Titus 1:14, nor associated with "genealogies" as in I Timothy 1:4. The term is thus left unrestricted to include all those religious aberrations which are the accompaniments of any turning away from the truth of the Gospel. Fairbairn remarks:

> There is enough of this itching after false doctrine in the scattered communities of Protestantism to humble and sadden any Christian heart; the signs of the times give no doubtful indication of even more yet to come;

but it is in the bosom of the great apostasy that the most marked and mournful exemplification of the apostle's prediction is to be met with.

b. The charge to a sober fulfillment of his ministry, vv. 5-8. With "but" Paul again makes the following charge emphatically personal by setting Timothy in contrast to the people just mentioned. He renews his charge (v. 5) and gives the basis for the charge (vv. 6-8).

1) The statement of the charge, v. 5. The heart of the duty urged is, "be thou sober in all things." The present tense denotes this as his standing duty, he must continue to do so. The verb "sober" is used literally as meaning "to abstain from wine," and then metaphorically to depict the condition of being alert, calm, and circumspect. He must keep his mind and actions free from that mental and spiritual intoxication experienced by those with morbid cravings for that which is sensational and novel.

The three imperatives which follow, again without connective particles, indicate the areas in which Timothy is to display his sobriety. "Suffer hardship," that is, ill treatment, what is bad. He will experience reproach and persecution but such experiences are not to becloud his sobriety. "Do the work of an evangelist." The manifold tasks, the harassing difficulties, the manifestations of antagonism must not distract him from his primary task of being "an evangelist," a bringer of God's good news. The term, used without an article, does not here designate a distinct office but rather characterizes him as one whose chief activity is the bringing of the good news of the Gospel of Christ. His ministry must be evangelistic in nature. In spite of toil and hardship, Timothy is urged, "fulfill thy ministry." He must carry it out to its end, complete all its demands and requirements. The Greek word for "ministry" speaks of Christian work in general, every mode of Christian service, and does not have the specialized significance which our word "ministry" has acquired.

2) The basis for the charge, vv. 6-8. At the beginning of verse 5 Timothy was set in contrast to the fickle people mentioned in verses 3 and 4, but in the latter part of the verse the thought shifts to the contrast between Timothy, still engaged in fulfilling his ministry, and Paul who has come to the termination of his ministry as set forth in verses 6-8. The example of Paul must motivate Timothy likewise to persevere until the end. The words "for I," the conjunction with the emphatic personal pronoun, mark this causal relationship. Timothy must diligently preach, not only because apostasy is coming (vv. 3, 4), but also because Paul's departure will leave him to carry on the work left by his beloved teacher and friend.

Verses 6-8 constitute one of the grandest testimonies in all ages to Christian victory in the face of impending death. They have made an indelible impression upon Christian hearts in all subsequent generations. His testimony deals with the present, the past, and the future. He depicts his present circumstances (v. 6), views his life in retrospect (v. 7), and rejoices in his prospects for the future (v. 8).

a) His appraisal of present circumstances, v. 6. "I am already being offered." The verb means "to pour out as a drink offering, to make a libation." The process has "already" begun. It began with his first trial before the court of Nero, while the final outcome, which was no longer in doubt, would be the shedding of his blood in martyrdom. But Paul does not speak of it by the grim term of death but rather pictures it as an offering. His whole life has been presented to God as a living sacrifice; now his death, comparable to the pouring out of the wine as the last act of the sacrificial ceremony, will complete the sacrifice. Paul employed the same figure in writing to the Philippians (2:17). What was then a grave possibility is now being faced as an impending certainty.

Paul adds a parallel statement, "and the time of my departure is come." He thought of his life's work as ended and his "departure" as at hand. The word "departure," a common expression for death, means "a loosing," and was used of loosening the tent cords when breaking camp or of hoisting the anchor of a ship about to sail. Either figure would be applicable here, but the word had apparently about lost the force of the figure and may here simply denote the act of leaving on a journey. "Paul prefers to think of death as the departure after a brief bivouac and the setting forth on another journey" (Pope). The verb rendered "is come" means "to stand by, to be on hand," and implies that death was already standing by, simply awaiting its time.

Such was Paul's evaluation of his present circumstances. But only one possessed of a vital faith and the assurance of a blessed future could make such an appraisal of his grim prospects. His language is ample proof of how little he feared the approach of the hour of death.

b) His life in retrospect, v. 7. From his consideration of present circumstances Paul turns to review the past. That past he summarizes under three concise statements. "I have fought the good fight." The figure is not drawn from the battlefield but from the well-known Greek games. It is the picture of an athlete struggling and contending for the prize. The underlying figure may be that of the wrestling match or the boxing arena. "I have fought the agonizing contest to a finish." His entire life as an apostle has been a ceaseless, strenuous conflict with Satan and his minions, with evil men and with forces of spiritual wickedness. In contrast to the struggles in the games, this has indeed been a "good," a noble, grand contest, the grandest contest in which man can engage, and the prize is of inestimable value. The use of the perfect tense, "I have fought," pictures the contest as having been pursued to the end and completed. He can now stop and look back upon it as finished. To the objection that this was not yet true for Paul, Hendriksen well replies:

> When death is very near and very certain, it is easy for the mind to project itself into that near-by future moment from which it then looks back upon the past, and rejoices not only in that past but in the present blessing which that past has produced.

In the second statement, "I have finished the course," the figure is specifically that of the foot race. His agitated apostolic career might well be compared to that of a strenuous race. With his eyes fixed upon the goal, he has been putting all of his energy into the race to win the prize (cf. Phil. 3:13, 14). Now the race has been completed and he rests at the goal as he looks back upon the successfully completed course.

With the words "I have kept the faith" he drops the figure and states the literal fact. Here apparently by "the faith" he does not mean merely his own personal faith in Christ but is thinking of the Gospel as the precious deposit that was entrusted to him. Amid the countless dangers encountered from active foes and false friends he has unflinchingly held to that Gospel and has guarded it against perversion or adulteration. Now he is ready to render account to Him who entrusted it to him.

To accuse Paul of vainglory in these assertions is seriously to misconceive the purpose of Paul's testimony. It is a charge worthy only of a rationalist. Paul is bearing witness to what God's grace has wrought in his life. Our translation might give an impression of egotism by placing the pronoun "I" at the beginning of each phrase. But Paul's emphasis is not on the pronouns but on the objects which are placed forward for the sake of emphasis, "the good fight," "the race," "the faith" standing first in each instance. With one foot in the grave and his heart already in Heaven, for a man like Paul such a testimony is not bragging but is a sincere testimony of actual accomplishment through God's grace to encourage Timothy. "The ring of triumph and noble self-assurance is intended to rouse Timothy, as the dying cry of a general inspires his flagging followers to new courage and daring" (Pope).

c) His prospects for the future, v. 8. From the past the apostle turns his eyes to the future and exults in what lies before him. "Henceforth," for what remains, "there is laid up for me the crown of righteousness." The victory has been won, the goal has been reached, what remains is the reward which "is laid up for" him, is safely stored away and kept safe for him. The reward is "the crown of righteousness." The meaning is not a crown which consists of righteousness, for our righteousness is not earned by strenuous effort. Rather, it is the crown which belongs to or is the due reward of righteousness. "It is that kind and measure of bliss which the wrestler in righteousness alone is either entitled or prepared to enjoy" (Fairbairn). This crown he will receive from "the Lord, the righteous judge." The appositional description of the Lord as "the righteous judge," or the umpire, continues the picture of the athletic games. The adjective "righteous" points to the fact that Christ as the umpire

112

will make no mistake and commit no injustice. Apparently there is an intended contrast here with the unrighteous worldly judge before whom Paul has just appeared. The time of the bestowal of the crown is "at that day," not at his death but at the time of the Lord's return. In that day when the hidden things shall be brought to light and the dark things shall be made plain, then the righteousness of the true believer will be displayed and the righteous judgments of God will be convincingly demonstrated.

But Paul hastens to add that this is "not to me only." It is a blessing which he is eager to share with others, namely, "all them that have loved his appearing." The perfect tense "have loved" denotes their habitual love and desire for His appearing. Paul does not say, "all them that have loved Him," but rather "his appearing." "Of all the indications that one loves the Lord, this earnest longing for His return is one of the best, for such a person is thinking not only of himself and of his own glory but also of his Lord and of the latter's public vindication. For all such persons the wreath is waiting" (Hendriksen). But Paul's words clearly exclude all those for whom the second coming of the Lord is a source of terror. Do we merely give assent to the doctrinal truth of His imminent return, or do we show by our daily life that we love, yearn for, and await His appearing?

THE CONCLUSION, 4:9-22

Give diligence to come shortly unto me: for Demas forsook me, having loved this present world, and went to Thessalonica; Crescens to Galatia, Titus to Dalmatia.

Only Luke is with me. Take Mark, and bring him with thee; for he is useful to me for ministering. But Tychicus I sent to Ephesus. The cloak that I left at Troas with Carpus, bring when thou comest, and the books, especially the parchments. Alexander the coppersmith did me much evil: the Lord will render to him according to his works: of whom do thou also beware; for he greatly withstood our words. At my first defense no one took my part, but all forsook me: may it not be laid to their account. But the Lord stood by me, and strengthened me; that through me the message might be fully proclaimed, and that all the Gentiles might hear: and I was delivered out of the mouth of the lion. The Lord will deliver me from every evil work, and will save me unto his heavenly kingdom: to whom be the glory forever and ever. Amen.

Salute Prisca and Aquila, and the house of Onesiphorus. Erastus remained at Corinth: but Trophimus I left at Melitus sick. Give diligence to come before winter. Eubulus saluteth thee, and Pudens, and Linus, and Claudia, and all the brethren.

The Lord be with thy spirit. Grace be with you. Amen.

THE EPISTLE CLOSES with several detached matters of a more personal nature. The conclusion consists of personal requests and items of information (vv. 9-18), parting salutations (vv. 19-21), and the closing benediction (v. 22).

1. *The Personal Requests and Items of Information,* vv. 9-18

Following his grand testimony in the face of impending death, the thoughts of the apostle turn once more to the immediate present with its many comparatively petty demands and circumstances. He expresses his loneliness and his desire for assistance (vv. 9-12), makes a request for his cloak and books (v. 13), informs and warns Timothy concerning Alexander (vv. 14, 15), and recounts his experience at his first defense (vv. 16-18).

a. His loneliness and his desire for assistance, vv. 9-12. Having been accustomed to a considerable group of co-workers around him during the years of his active missionary labors, the apostle keenly feels his loneliness now in his dank dungeon. He requests Timothy to come to him (v. 9), explains concerning some of his companions (vv. 10, 11a), asks that Mark be brought along (v. 11b), and mentions the commission given Tychicus (v. 12).

1) The request for Timothy to come quickly, v. 9. "Give diligence to come shortly unto me." He has previously hinted at his yearning to see Timothy (1:4, 8), now he states the request. In the face of approaching death the apostle craves the presence and sympathy of his "beloved child" Timothy. And so he urges him, "Give diligence," make haste, exert every energy to come "shortly," or quickly. Yet it is clear from what follows that his request was not prompted merely by his sentimental attachment to Timothy. There was ample reason for this request. His presence was needed.

2) The explanation concerning his companions, vv. 10, 11a. He is lonely and in need of Timothy because most of his companions have left him. "For Demas forsook me" records a poignant fact. Having been his trusted fellow-worker during the first imprisonment (Col. 4:14; Philemon 24), Paul must now sadly relate that he "forsook me." The original double compound verb means to forsake one who is in a set of adverse circumstances, to leave in the lurch, to abandon, to let down. Demas has let him down and abandoned him in an hour of need. The tense points to a severance of his connection with Paul at a definite crisis; the precise circumstances are left

unexplained. The reason for the departure is that he "loved this present world." The tense of the original indicates that he has "fallen in love with the present age," that is, "the earthly, visible world, with its good things, in opposition to the invisible, still future kingdom of Christ, which was the object of the highest love of Paul, and for the sake of which he endured willingly the heaviest affliction" (Van Oosterzee). His love for the present age evidently is set in contrast to those who "have loved his appearing" (v. 8). Demas is not charged with forsaking Christ, and the words do not prove that Demas became an apostate from Christianity. But the sin was a grievous one, a self-interest which made him unwilling any longer to be associated with the apostle because of the dangers involved. As Ellicott says: "He loved safety and ease and the fleeting pleasures of this world, and had not the Christian fortitude to share the dangers, or the Christian love to minister to the sufferings, of the nearly desolate apostle." Unfortunately there are too many Christians today who seek to shirk the discomforts and dangers of an uncompromising stand for Christ and desire to enjoy the ease and pleasures of life instead. Having broken with Paul, Demas "went to Thessalonica." Why he went there we can only conjecture.

Two other companions are no longer with Paul. "Crescens to Galatia, Titus to Dalmatia." Paul is not censuring their absence, although the absence of a separate verb has raised the question whether they left on some errand of their own accord or had been sent by Paul. Probably the latter. Certainly no blame is attached to their absence but is mentioned to explain Paul's loneliness. "Crescens," of whom we have no further information, has gone to "Galatia." Apparently the reference is to the Roman province of Galatia in Asia Minor, but a few manuscrips read

"Gaul," the European Gaul. If Paul has made a trip to Spain, such a trip to Gaul by one of his assistants is quite intelligible. Titus has gone to "Dalmatia," lying on the eastern shores of the Adriatic. The reference shows that Titus had not been stationed permanently on Crete as its first bishop.

Thus Paul is almost alone. "Only Luke is with me." He alone of his intimate friends and usual companions is left at the apostle's side. And what a comfort he was to Paul! As "the beloved physician" (Col. 4:14) he was Paul's doctor, friend, and fellow worker. Apparently he wrote this letter for Paul. He had been with Paul during his first Roman imprisonment and now he appears with him again, faithful until the end.

3) The instructions concerning Mark, v. 11b. "Take Mark, and bring him with thee." He is to "pick up" Mark and in company with him make the journey to Rome. This shows that Mark was in the vicinity; perhaps he was now assisting Timothy in his work in the churches of Asia. Mark is needed at Rome; the condition of the Christian cause at Rome called for his coming. Hence Paul adds, "for he is useful to me for ministering." Mark has redeemed himself and fully regained the confidence and trust of Paul. Paul has found him "useful," serviceable "for ministering." The reference may be to personal service to Paul or to public service in the cause of Christ at Rome. The context favors the latter.

4) The commission to Tychicus, v. 12. "But Tychicus I sent to Ephesus." Tychicus was a native of Asia and Paul's traveling companion during the latter part of the third missionary journey (Acts 20:4) and was the bearer of the letters to the Ephesians and the Colossians (Eph. 6:21; Col. 4:7) during the Acts 28 imprisonment. Since we cannot assume that II Timothy is con-

temporaneous with those epistles, this mission of Tychicus to Ephesus must be later and implies that Paul experienced two separate imprisonments at Rome. As Paul's trusted emissary Tychicus is now "sent," or commissioned, to Ephesus. The verb is best regarded as an epistolary aorist, whereby the writer places himself in point of time in the position of the receiver instead of the writer of the letter. In English we would use the present, "I am sending." He is sending Tychicus to take the place of Timothy and Mark during their absence in Rome. Then naturally Tychicus would also deliver this letter to Timothy. The mention of Ephesus then does not mean that Timothy was away from that city but rather that Tychicus would replace him there.

b. His request for his cloak and books, v. 13. The coming of Timothy is to be used to supply Paul's personal needs as well. "The cloak that I left at Troas with Carpus, bring when thou comest." This statement, plainly implying a recent visit to Troas by Paul, cannot be fitted into the Acts narrative and thus forbids any view that this epistle was written during the Acts 28 imprisonment. That Timothy is ordered to stop there on his way to Rome again points to Ephesus as his place of residence. From Ephesus Timothy would go to Troas, cross over to Greece, follow the Egnatian Way to Dyrrachium, sail to Brundisium, and thence overland to Rome.

Shivering in his damp dungeon, Paul longs for his "cloak" to ward off the cold, specially in view of the approaching winter (v. 21). This "cloak" was a circular cape made of heavy material, apparently without sleeves, with only an opening for the head in the center. It was used as an outer garment for protection against cold and rain. It has been asserted that the mention of such matters was beneath the dignity of an inspired letter. Rather it shows us that inspiration is not indifferent to the so-called trivial things of life. As Kelly remarks:

It is good for our souls to believe that God takes a personal interest even in so small a matter. Where God is left out, even saints become a prey to personal vanity or worldly fashion.

This request has been held to be inconsistent with the preceding statement about Paul's impending death, that Paul has already taken his final farewell of Timothy and does not expect to see him again. Admittedly the objection has force. But would a forger have dared to insert such a request here and thus run the danger of creating a suspicious difficulty? But the request is psychologically probable if it was written by Paul. As Harwood points out, it is a well-known fact that "even when men know they must die soon, and are entirely resigned to death, nevertheless they frequently speak of things, and of their affairs, as if they expected life to move on as usual" (Lange *Commentary*). If we accept the implication of verse 16 that the letter was written between his first and second appearing before the imperial court, and that an indefinite time period intervened, the request of Paul is quite natural.

The desire behind the request made to Timothy was not restricted to his physical comfort, for he adds, "and the books, especially the parchments." "The books" would contain writings on the cheaper and more perishable papyrus paper, while "the parchments" have reference to writings considered of higher importance since they were written on the costlier and more permanent skins of vellum. The question as to the contents of these books and parchments has taxed the ingenuity of the commentators, and the conjectures have varied considerably. That rolls of the Old Testament Scriptures were among them seems obvious. Whatever their contents, Paul's desire now for his books is inspiring. Even as an old man facing certain death, the apostle has not lost his interest for study and mental pursuits. It presents a standing challenge to the minister to be an indefatigable student, especially of the Word of God.

c. His information and warning concerning Alexander, vv. 14, 15. "Alexander the coppersmith did me much evil." This Alexander, a determined opponent, is identified as "the coppersmith," or more generally, "the metal worker." It seems unlikely that he is the man mentioned in I Timothy 1:20, for then the proper identification would be by his explusion, not his trade. He has publicly withstood Paul both in deed (v. 14) and word (v. 15). Apparently he was one of Paul's accusers before the imperial court, "for he greatly withstood our words." He was able to damage Paul's defense in the eyes of the judges. In view of the bitter opposition which he has displayed, Paul adds, "the Lord will render to him according to his works." Instead of desiring personal vengeance, Paul leaves the matter of retribution to the Lord. Manuscript authority favors the future indicative reading, rather than the optative of wish. It is not an imprecation upon him but a calm forecast of his coming judgment from the evidence of his works. He has been an aggressive, persistent, and vicious opponent, hence Timothy is told, "of whom do thou also beware."

d. His experience at his "first defense," vv. 16-18. "At my first defense no one took my part, but all forsook me." Some scholars think that Paul now grows reminiscent and refers back to his first imprisonment and appearance before the imperial court. That is possible, but as we read the words it seems rather that he is giving Timothy fresh information, not something that occurred some three years before. Neither is there any evidence to think that at that time "all forsook him," leaving him in a lurch. We regard the reference as being to the first phrase of his trial now before the imperial court.

His "defense" (*apologia*) was his speech of self-defense in response to the indictment lodged against him. The reference to his "first" defense may mean that a twofold charge was laid against him, namely, complicity in the burning of Rome, and "treason, shown by hostility to the established customs of society, and by weakening the Imperial authority."[1] He had been vindicated on the first charge but the hostility of the court left no doubt as to the outcome on the second charge, to be heard later. Better is the view that the trial took place in two stages. At his first defense Paul's bold presentation of his own case made such an impression that the evidence was held to be inconclusive, Paul was remanded to jail, and the case adjourned to allow more proof to be accumulated for a second hearing. But the attitude of the court left no doubt as to the final outcome. An indefinite period of time would then ensue between the two stages of the trial. He now writes after the first appearing before the court.

1) The absence of patron friends, v. 16. Paul informs Timothy that "no one took my part, but all forsook me." There were no willing advocates to plead his cause, no patrons with standing before the court willing to appear in his behalf. Apparently even his witnesses failed him (see under 1:15). They "all forsook" him. Paul was deeply disappointed but he generously forgave them and prayed that it might "not be laid to their account." He recognized the magnitude of the danger to which such an exhibition of their friendship in that hour would ex-

---

1. W. M. Ramsay, *St. Paul the Traveller and the Roman Citizen*, (1896), p. 361.

pose them. Christianity, now distinguished from Judaism, was regarded as an illegal religion and to espouse the cause of its chief exponent was indeed personally dangerous. With no one to appear on his behalf, Alexander's opposition carried great weight.

2) The strengthening presence of the Lord, v. 17. "But the Lord stood by me," stood at his side as his helper and friend. The Lord filled him with power, lifted him above cringing fear, and gave him boldness to present his cause. The intended result of this strengthening was "that through me the message might be fully proclaimed, and that all the Gentiles might hear." The very occasion gave Paul an opportunity to fulfill his commission of proclaiming the message of Christ, and that in the very heart of the empire before the highest earthly tribunal. It afforded an opportunity for the vast crowd of Gentiles who were attracted to the trial to hear Paul's presentation of his message. He clearly set forth the content of his message, thus showing that it was no dangerous or subversive movement which he represented.

The result of that bold self-defense was that he escaped immediate condemnation. "I was delivered out of the mouth of the lion." The impression of Paul's defense made immediate condemnation impossible, and the case was recessed to allow time for further investigation. Various have been the conjectures as to the meaning of the "lion,"—literal lions in the amphitheater, Nero, or Satan. The original does not have the definite article and the emphasis is on his rescue *"out of"* the lion's *mouth*. It seems best to take the expression as meaning deliverance from great danger.

3) The assurance concerning the future, v. 18. The experience of past deliverance assures him of future deliverance. "The Lord will deliver me from every evil

work." Some would give "evil work" a subjective meaning as denoting his own temptation to sin or to lose heart and fail his Lord, but that seems improbable here. The evil works are the vicious activities of his enemies. He is not expecting deliverance from death, but, as the changed proposition in the original suggests (*apo* instead of *ek*), he is assured of the removal *from the presence of* "every evil work," and that through death. He will be delivered from the machinations of every form of evil through the gates of martyrdom. For God "will save me unto his heavenly kingdom," thus completing the salvation.

The contemplation of what the Lord has done and will do fills his soul with praise, giving birth to a doxology, "to whom be the glory forever and ever. Amen." The doxology is here unmistakably addressed to Christ and is another proof of Paul's conviction concerning the deity of Christ. The solemn "Amen" seals his personal ratification of this glorious hope.

2. *The Personal Greetings, vv. 19-21*

Personal greetings are appended. "Salute Prisca and Aquila." The words indicate that this Christian couple, last heard of as being in Rome (Rom. 16:3), has returned to Ephesus. Their long friendship has lastingly endeared them to Paul and he thinks first of them. Their names are mentioned six times in the New Testament and always together. Here as usual the name of Prisca (a form always used by Paul) stands first [2] As to the reason for the order we can only conjecture. Whatever the reason, Prisca is a worthy member of that noble band of Christian women who have done so much for the cause of Christ.

Paul also sends greetings to "the house of Onesiphor-

2. Four out of six times her name is given first (Acts 18:18, 26; Rom. 16:3; II Tim. 4:19).

us." (See the discussion under 1:16-18.) The reference again seems to imply Timothy's residence at Ephesus.

Paul explains the absence of two companions whom Timothy would expect to be with Paul. "Erastus remained at Corinth." Perhaps he is Paul's companion in travel (Acts 19:22) rather than the treasurer of the city of Corinth with whom Paul stayed when he wrote Romans (Rom. 16:23). Why he stayed at Corinth is not indicated. As to the second companion, Paul remarks, "Trophimus I left at Melitus sick." Here again is a note which cannot be fitted into the story of Paul's travels as recorded in Acts and necessitates the assumption of two imprisonments. Harvey points out that this passing reference "clearly shows that miracles of healing were not wrought at the mere will, even of an apostle, they were doubtless exceptional manifestations of divine power, made only as the Holy Spirit directed and empowered him who performed them."

Again Paul repeats his request for Timothy's coming, now adding "before winter" (v. 21). If the journey were delayed travel would be dangerous or even made impossible, since during the winter months all navigation on the Mediterranean closed down.

Greetings are sent from four people at Rome. "Eubulus saluteth thee, and Pudens, and Linus, and Claudia." They are all new names, Christians at Rome who have made contact with Paul, and not his intimate companions. Concerning the first name not even tradition has anything to say. Linus may perhaps be the man who became bishop of the church at Rome. Attempted identifications of the other two are very improbable.

"And all the brethren" perhaps means all those Christians in Rome whom Paul has been in touch with through Luke.

3. The Closing Benediction, v. 22

The epistle closes with a double benediction. "The Lord be with thy spirit" is Paul's personal benediction upon Timothy, his last word to him. In the second part, "grace be with you" ("you" in the plural), Timothy is united with all believers who are with him at Ephesus.

BIBLIOGRAPHY ON II TIMOTHY

Alford, Henry, *The Greek Testament.* Vol. III. CHICAGO: Moody Press (1958 reprint).

Bernard, J. H., "The Pastoral Epistles," *Cambridge Greek Testament.* Cambridge: Cambridge University Press (1922 reprint), lxxviii and 192 pp.

Boise, James Robinson, *Notes, Critical and Explanatory on the Greek Text of Paul's Epistles.* Ed., Nathan E. Wood. Boston: Silver, Burdett & Co. (1896), 582 pp.

Brown, Ernest Faulkner, "The Pastoral Epistles," *Westminster Commentaries.* London: Methuen & Co., Ltd. (1917), xxxiv and 121 pp.

Ellicott, Charles J., *A Critical and Grammatical Commentary on the Pastoral Epistles.* Andover: Warren F. Draper (1865), xviii and 265 pp.

Erdman, Charles R., *The Pastoral Epistles of Paul.* Philadelphia: The Westminster Press (1923), 158 pp.

Fairbairn, Patrick, *Commentary on the Pastoral Epistles.* Grand Rapids: Zondervan Publishing House (1956 reprint), ix and 451 pp.

Greene, J. P., "The Pastoral Epistles, 1st and 2nd Timothy, Titus," *The Convention Series.* Nashville: S. S. Board, Southern Baptist Convention (1915), 210 pp.

Harvey, H., "Commentary on the Pastoral Epistles, First and Second Timothy and Titus; and the Epistle to Philemon," *An American Commentary on the New Testament.* Philadelphia: The American Baptist Publication Society (1890; reprint, no date), 164 pp.

Hendriksen, William, "Exposition of the Pastoral Epistles," *New Testament Commentary*. Grand Rapids: Baker Book House (1957), 404 pp.

Horton, R. F., "The Pastoral Epistles," *The Century Bible*. London: Blackwood, Le Bas & Co. (no date), 196 pp.

Humphreys, A. E., "The Epistles to Timothy and Titus," *The Cambridge Bible for Schools*. Cambridge: Cambridge University Press (1925 reprint), 271 pp.

Huther, Joh. Ed., "Critical and Exegetical Handbook to the Epistles of St. Paul to Timothy and Titus," Meyer's *Critical and Exegetical Commentary on the New Testament*. Translated by David Hunter. Edinburgh: T. & T. Clark (1893), 379 pp.

Kelly, William, *An Exposition of the Two Epistles to Timothy*. London: C. A. Hammond (no date), xv and 348 pp.

Lenski, R. C. H., *The Interpretation of St. Paul's Epistles to the Colossians, to the Thessalonians, to Timothy, to Titus and to Philemon*. Columbus, Ohio: Lutheran Book Concern (1937), 986 pp.

Lilley, J. P., "The Pastoral Epistles," *Handbooks for Bible Classes*. Edinburgh: T. & T. Clark (1901), 255 pp.

Lipscomb, David, *A Commentary on the New Testament Epistles*. Edited, with additional Notes, by J. W. Shepherd. Nashville: Gospel Advocate Co. (1942), 324 pp.

Lock, Walter, "A Critical and Exegetical Commentary on the Pastoral Epistles," *The International Critical Commentary*. Edinburgh: T. & T. Clark (1924; 1936 reprint), xliv and 163 pp.

Moule, H. C. G., "The Second Epistle to Timothy," *Devotional Commentaries*. London: The Religious

Tract Society (1905), 192 pp.

Pope, R. Martin, *The Epistles of Paul the Apostle to Timothy and Titus.* London: Charles H. Kelly (1901), 248 pp.

Scott, E. F., "The Pastoral Epistles," *The Moffatt New Testament Commentary.* London: Hodder and Stoughton (1936; 1948 reprint), xxxviii and 186 pp.

Spence, H. D. M., "The Pastoral Epistles of St. Paul," *Ellicott's Commentary on the Whole Bible.* Grand Rapids: Zondervan Publishing House (reprint, no date), pp. 171-264.

Van Oosterzee, J. J., "The Pastoral Epistles, The Second Epistle of Paul to Timothy," Lange *Commentary on the Holy Scriptures,* Translated by Drs. Washburn and Harwood. Grand Rapids: Zondervan Publishing House (reprint, no date), pp. 77-120.

White, Newport J. D., "The First and Second Epistles to Timothy and the Epistle to Titus," *The Expositor's Greek Testament.* Grand Rapids: Wm. B. Eerdmans Publishing Co. (reprint, no date), pp. 55-202.

Williams, Charles B., *A Commentary on the Pauline Epistles.* Chicago: Moody Press (1953), 507 pp.

Wuest, Kenneth S., *The Pastoral Epistles in the Greek New Testament for the English Reader.* Grand Rapids: Wm. B. Eerdmans Publishing Co. (1952), 209 pp.